DESIGNING PATCH DYNAMICS

Editors: Brian McGrath · Victoria Marshall · M.L. Cadenasso ·
J. Morgan Grove · S.T.A. Pickett · Richard Plunz · Joel Towers

COLUMBIA UNIVERSITY GRADUATE SCHOOL OF ARCHITECTURE, PLANNING AND PRESERVATION
MASTERS OF SCIENCE IN ARCHITECTURE AND URBAN DESIGN PROGRAM

Designing Patch Dynamics was produced at Columbia University
Graduate School of Architecture, Planning and Preservation
Office of the Dean, Mark Wigley and the director of print publications,
Jeannie Kim.

Urban Design: Brian McGrath, Victoria Marshall, Joel Towers

Urban Design Students 2002: Marc Brossa, Yu-Heng
Chiang, Kratma Saini, Pavithra Sriprakash, John Tran

Urban Design Students 2003: Atiq Ahmed, Peter Allen, Nicolas
Bacigalupo, Benjamin Batista-Roman, Paul Blaer, Andrew Brotzman,
Flora Hsiang-I Chen, Poku Chen, Chi-Yu Chou, Joseph Chi-Yu Chou, Kim
DeFreitas, E. Scott Elder, Emilia Ferri, Manolo Figueroa, Karl Hamilton,
Vivian Hernandez, Chin-Hua Huang, Esi-Kilanga Ifeytayo Bowser, Van
Tsing Hung Joseph, Olivia Li-Chun Kuo, Pei-lun Lin, Derek Mizner,
Justin G. Moore,Joseph Plouffe, Matthew Priest, Timothy Reed, Peter
Robinson, Marjan Sansen, Gupreet Shah, Christopher Small, Angela
Chen-Mai Soong, Pavi Sriprakash, Keunsook Suk, Amit Talwar, Camellia
Han Tian, Oliver Valle, Ward Leo Jan Verbakel, Jenny Jie Zhou, Jiang Zhu

Architecture: Richard Plunz

Architecture Students 2002: Brian Abell, Tomasz Adach, Katherine Chang,
Sari Kronish, Raphael Levy, Carolyn Walls, Mariam Mojdehi, Keith Tsang

Design by Andrea Hyde for Honest, stayhonest.com

Layout by Alanna Talty and Phanat Sonemangkhala, phanat.net

Copy Editors: Alanna Talty and Karen Hock

Published by the Graduate School of Architecture, Planning and
   Preservation of Columbia University, New York, NY 10027,
   in collaboration with The USDA Forest Service Northern
   Research Station and The Institute of Ecosystem Studies.

ISBN 1-883584-47-7

   Library of Congress Cataloging-in-Publication Data

Designing patch dynamics / edited by Brian McGrath ... [et al.].
     p. cm. -- (New urbanisms ; 10)
 Includes bibliographical references.
 ISBN 978-1-883584-47-4
1. Architecture--Environmental aspects. 2. Architectural design. 3. City
planning. 4. Human ecology. I. McGrath, Brian. II. Columbia University.
Graduate School of Architecture, Planning, and Preservation.
NA2542.35.D47 2007
720'.47--dc22

Printed in Canada.

CONTENTS

INTRODUCTION

VICTORIA MARSHALL, BRIAN MCGRATH, AND JOEL TOWERS

In the summer of 2002, Drs. Steward T.A. Pickett, Mary L. Cadenasso, and J. Morgan Grove, scientists from the Baltimore Ecosystem Study (BES), approached Brian McGrath at the Urban Design Program at Columbia University's Graduate School of Architecture, Planning, and Preservation (GSAPP) with an innovative cross-disciplinary collaborative opportunity. Funded by the National Science Foundation's Long-Term Ecological Research Program (LTER), the BES brings together researchers from a variety of social and biophysical science disciplines to engage in data collection, education, and community outreach. Their primary goal is to understand and explain metropolitan Baltimore as a complex ecological system. In an intrepid and prescient next step for BES and LTER, Drs. Pickett, Cadenasso and Grove put forth the radical proposition that urban designers can help to break new ground in the field of ecology and that current ecosystem science would enliven our own design milieu. As we developed this New York based studio in partnership with BES, we have situated the disciplines of architecture and urban design within expanded discursive and geographic fields, gradually broadening the scope of inquiry to consider spatial, social, economic, and ecological dynamics throughout the entire northeastern coastal megalopolis.

This new alliance benefits from both the resources within Columbia University and our specific professional experience as architects, landscape architects, and urban designers. During the last decade, the GSAPP, particularly the Urban Design Program, significantly augmented the population and diversity of its students by drawing post-graduate architects from every corner of the world. A substantial University investment in the paperless studio model initiated by former Dean Bernard Tschumi, the renewed global attraction of New York City, and a rising interest in the creative potential of contemporary urban design all contributed to a new wave of talented students crowding the studios of the one-year Master of Science in Architecture and Urban Design. Simultaneously, the GSAPP has increasingly recruited a new generation of design professionals to teach as adjunct studio critics, creating a dynamically heterogeneous socio-cultural ecosystem poised between academia and professional practice. As a result, the Urban Design Studio has become an innovative pedagogical experiment in directing networked transdisciplinary and transnational knowledge towards understanding urbanism at the turn of the 21st century.

The GSAPP has recently distinguished itself by creating design studios that current Dean Mark Wigley calls "experimental laboratories." Our studio forges ahead as a field experiment, taking graduates from architecture programs from around the world into a North American ecological as well as urban context. The results of the first two years of collaboration with the BES are presented in this studio work folio, marking the beginning of a long term partnership in designing, researching, writing, and teaching together in an urban ecology research lab we call the Urban Field Station. This Field Station, a project of the USDA Forest Service Northern Research Station, will foster future design explorations to test the lessons learned in our Baltimore studio in other sites along the northeastern seaboard and abroad.

Pedagogical Framework

The BES/GSAPP studio is situated between large-scale environmental trends and localized social behaviors accompanying the worldwide shift in urban economies from regional centers of industrial production towards global networks of symbolic and material processing – a trend Manuel Castells has called the "emergence of an urban society without cities" (1999). Geopolitical, technological, and economic restructurings have unleashed rapid urbanization throughout vast areas of the globe, and are outpacing earth's evolutionary time frames. Previous distinctions such as "city" and "nature" are complicated within this vastly dispersed environment with millions of megalopolitan nomads moving between housing and work, and between leisure and consumption. Periods of economic crisis and urban restructuring are now increasingly more frequent than those brief moments of generalized expansion along a definite developmental path. Conditions change before our bodies and psyches can adjust; the extent of change reaches beyond the control of political and social organizations at all scales. Each student who comes to our program has lived through these transformations from the unique perspective of his or her own life experiences, further strengthening our project's global implications.

What is the role of architecture and urban design in this chaotic context of global change? How can such a diverse assemblage of students and faculty make a contribution in a short period of time? Our experimental framework and methodology are based on the premise that urban designers must reach beyond the current boundaries of contemporary practice and academia, as well as beyond our training as architects. Rosalind Krauss's study of art practices in the 1960s and 1970s serves as a model for reinvigorating our urban design studio by capitalizing on the lack of clear disciplinary definition. Our way of working resembles what Gary Genosko has called "transdiciplinary metamethodologies" (2002), wherein we continue to evolve new processes and ways of thinking, working, and building that are collaborative, improvisational, and experimental – and at odds with established institutional and disciplinary systems. Transdisciplinarity does not follow the predictable path of interdisciplinary practices which typically simply transfer the working methods of one established field to another without a critical shift in thought. Metamethodologies require developing a sense of alterity; we must be simultaneously immersed within the expertise of a working methodology, but at the same time maintain an openness and self-consciousness outside of single methodological and epistemological frameworks.

Ways of Seeing

At the start of the fall semester in 2002, the GSAPP hosted a seminar entitled "Ways of Seeing." Building on John Berger's book of the same name, the transdisciplinary event initiated a conversation across discursive boundaries to establish a rich, multivalent foundation for the subsequent design studio. Significantly influenced by Walter Benjamin's seminal essay, "The Work of Art in the Age of Mechanical Reproduction," Berger presents culturally constructed frames of reference as constraints on understanding and imagination. He illustrates these limitations through explorations of two-dimensional modes of production and reproduction. Perhaps most importantly, Berger adds to Benjamin's text the temporal sensibility of a "televisual" age attempting to reconcile the increasing speed of communication and its impact on cultural transformation (1972). The seminar discussion featured architectural historian Kenneth Frampton, geographer David Harvey, cultural theorist May Joseph, and Dr. Pickett of the BES, with architectural historian and activist Jean Gardner as moderator. An effort to situate and program urban design practice emerged from their conversation.

The practice of urban design operates at the scale of very large systems described partly by patch dynamics - "the idea that communities are a mosaic of different areas (patches) within which nonbiological disturbances (such as climate) and biological interactions proceed" (Mac 1998). Change over time is a predominant factor. Alternately, urban design may be conceived at the much smaller scale of the body, differentiated by particularity and locality. Between these scales, distinct and interrelated temporal conditions are also at play. Strategic urban design responds to all of these competing and often contradictory concepts of place. Abstraction and conceptualization can help to see beyond the particularity of place, thereby extending spatial and temporal horizons. The negotiation among the tangible, performative, immediate projects of urban design, their long term transformative potential, and the dynamic processes of their production present what we consider to be a dialectical condition of urbanism. Emerging from a diverse array of disciplines, our definition of the study of urbanism suggests ways in which differently scaled and potentially conflicting discourses can expand the delineation of an urban design site and program.

The "Ways of Seeing" symposium was a provocation. Translating this into a design investigation in this first phase of the semester, we employed a spatiotemporal dialectic as a means of situating urban design practice between space (landscape) and time (system). In *Spaces of Hope*, David

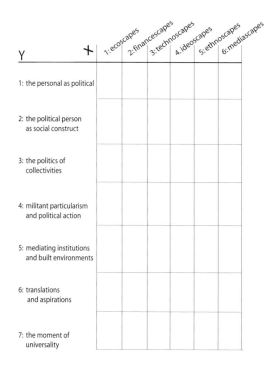

Y ✗

X-axis headers: 1: ecoscapes, 2: financescapes, 3: technoscapes, 4: ideoscapes, 5: ethnoscapes, 6: mediascapes

Y-axis rows:
1: the personal as political
2: the political person as social construct
3: the politics of collectivities
4: militant particularism and political action
5: mediating institutions and built environments
6: translations and aspirations
7: the moment of universality

Figure 1. The guiding matrix that emerged from David Harvey's "theaters" from *Spaces of Hope* plotted on the "y" axis and Arjun Appadurai's "-scapes" from *Modernity at Large* with our own addition of "ecoscapes" on the "x" axis.

Figure 2 (opposite). Resilience Models. Adapted from van der Leeuw, Sander E. and Chr. Aschan Leygonie. 2000. A Long Term Perspective on Resilience in Socio-Natural Systems. Abisko, Sweden.

Harvey identifies seven different theaters of action that for him represent "simultaneous and loosely coordinated shifts in both thinking and action across several scales" (2000) (Figure 1). The students were asked to explore how they might occupy and transform these theaters in order to site discursive fields within the broad context of regional and global discussions currently shaping perceptions and expectations about urban programs. Could this spatiotemporal model lead to mapping strategies that would enable them, as emerging urban designers, to see the relationships between physical site definition (spatial form) and the way we talk about and imagine a place (temporal process)? While Harvey's theaters of insurgent activity provided a starting point for a dialectical construction of space and time in an urban context of existing and emerging constituencies, a complex definition of "landscape" was still needed. Specific design propositions for each of the semester's given sites would ultimately be considered.

Next, we set Harvey's theaters in relation to Arjun Appadurai's multivalent construction of "scapes" from his 1996 book *Modernity at Large* (Figure 1). The relationship between each theater and Appadurai's landscape matrix was described historically (temporally) and territorially (spatially). A partial list of foci emerged concerning industrial and post-industrial economies, the evolution of capital, changes in the natural conditions of the site, and new models of self-organization. Students explored what happened in the past and speculated as to what would happen next. Theaters crossed over sites, offering points of comparison. The pedagogical position of the studio and the associated working methodology were intended to activate two realms of inquiry. First, by inserting urban design into an expanded field of urbanism, we were able to critically question the presumptions about site and program "realities" as they evolve over time. Secondly, by pursuing strategic urban designs that arose through frequent contact with various constituencies in multiple landscapes, we employed a dynamic and cross-disciplinary model. Working in this manner compelled constant redefinition of what constituted both site boundaries and programmatic restraints.

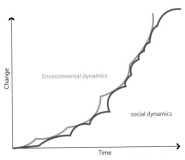

Resilience Diagram I. 'The relation between an independent, incrementally changing, environmentaly dynamic and cyclically changing cognitive dynamic with an invariant clock speed. The resilience of the relationship is inversely proportional to the vertical distance between the two curves. In this case, the system rapidly loses all resilience because the information-processing system does not adapt itself to the changes in the environmental dynamic.'

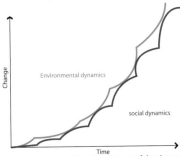

Resilience Diagram II. 'In this graph we have assumed that the existence of the changes in the environment increases regularly with each cycle. The resilience is, again inversely proportional to the vertical distance at any point in time. That distance still goes to infinity and resilience to zero, but after a larger number of time-steps because the changes in the information-processing system increase with each cycle of that system.'

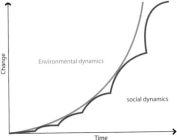

Resilience Diagram III. 'Resilience can be further improved by adapting the speed and frequency of change in social dynamics to the rate of environmental change. Very complex curves will result from this process, which reflect highly complex interactions, but which allow resilience to remain sufficient for a long time.'

Our interest was, in part, in making the realization of urban design processes transparent and multi-operational by exploring and enacting economic and social shifts spatially and temporally across sites in a performative rather than representational manner. To facilitate dialogue, we attempted to construct an interdisciplinary means of communicating design ideas with the many actors involved in urban decision making. By seeing this as a collaborative process, we hope to enlarge the possibilities of urban design thinking. It is on this last point that the quotations from Harvey and Berger intertwine with the specific structure established by this studio and the practice of urban design. By working together with residents and neighborhood groups, ecologists, and policy specialists, we were able to address many social and spatial themes that might otherwise have proven problematic. For example, the intersection of landscape, community, urban design, and ecology resulted in projects that challenge perceived notions of urban design. This is central not only to our work, but to the future of urban design practice.

Resilient Practices

Urban ecology as a paradigm is equally compelling. This view suggests that ecology and other more interactive frameworks represent a world view, and that the transformations associated with this "way of seeing" are essential reconfigurations in human-nature relations. In a paper presented at a workshop on system shock and system resilience, van der Leeuw and Aschan-Leygonie argue for just such paradigmatic change (Figure 2 & 3).

> "… [T]here is no 'social system,' and neither is there a 'natural system;' there are only socio-natural interactions. It thus becomes possible to talk about 'socio-natural relations' and 'socio-natural problems,' rather than about the relationship between social and natural systems, stressing the interactions while accepting the differences in the nature of their dynamics. Evidence is mounting that most, if not all, of the 'environmental' problems we encounter are exacerbated by the 'nature – culture' opposition in our minds. In separating ourselves from what we consider to be 'nature,' we have tended to favour [sic] human intervention in the natural domain as the way to 'solve' such 'environmental' problems --including saving our environment from ourselves" (van der Leeuw and others 2000).

A growing awareness of this issue has triggered a shift in the debate on environmental matters in the scientific arena, but increasingly also in the political agenda and in the eyes of the general public. Long-term urban ecosystem study is a relatively new field of research and provides a compelling argument for precisely the model of investigation and urban design explored in this studio. In describing urban ecology, Pickett writes:

> "There are the same basic kinds of interactions in cities as in other ecosystems. But those interactions are greatly affected not only by the structures that people have built and the energy they import, but also by people's cultures, behaviors, social organization and economy. So cities are just a somewhat more complicated kind of ecosystem, and new interactions among researchers will be required to understand cities as ecosystems. Ecologists, social scientists, economists, and engineers are all involved, along with city, county, state and national agencies. Interactions with the citizens and with community groups are also a big part of the success of an urban

ecosystem study. In spite of the fact that a majority of the U.S. population lives in metropolitan areas, ecologists have not studied cities and their surrounding suburban and rural lands as ecological systems. There are some isolated studies of specific factors, but the integrated studies to examine biodiversity, nutrient and energy flow, ecological structure, and dynamics of all these things through time, have not been done. In addition, if we apply a truly ecological perspective, the social, hydrological, atmospheric, and built components of the systems must also be included. All the disciplines required for this complete ecological understanding of an urban area have not been pulled together in a focused study before. This is cutting edge research" (Pickett 2005).

Choosing between urban ecology as practice or as paradigm seems particularly unwise. It is not clear whether environmental degradation and non-sustainable cultural and consumerist patterns can be resolved through adaptive transformations of practice alone. Equally unclear is how the transformation of social and economic structures would be achieved through the emergence of an ecological paradigm. Large-scale changes of the environment and social systems currently underway are indicative of how we see ourselves and our culture. They are also the result of patterns of consumption and the practice of making at many scales. This is the territory and responsibility of urban design. The relationship of urban design to social responsibility remains contested ground, raising more questions than it answers. To whom and for what are urban designers responsible? Is it the practice, the practitioners, or both that bear a social responsibility? Who is included or excluded when we say "social?" And what is the responsibility of society toward urban design?

Threads

This publication is organized like the studio itself, as a dialogue between design and science. Chapters alternate between these two voices, which

Pre-1980's	1980's	1990's
Culture is natural	Nature is cultural	Nature and culture have a reciprocal relationship
Humans are re-active to the environment	Humans are pro-active in the environment	Humans are inter-active with the environment
Environment is dangerous to humans	Humans are dangerous for the environment	Neither are dangerous if handled carefully
Environmental crises hit humans	Environmental crises are caused by humans	Environmental crises are caused by socio-natural interaction
Adaptation	Sustainability	Resilience
Apply technofixes	No new technology	Minimalist, balanced use of technology
'Milieu' perspective dominates	'Environment' perspective dominates	Attempts to balance both perspectives

Figure 3. Changing idea of nature. Adapted from van der Leeuw, Sander E. and Chr. Aschan Leygonie. 2000. A Long Term Perspective on Resilience in Socio-Natural Systems. Abisko, Sweden.

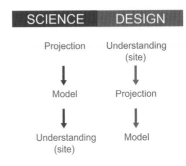

Figure 4. Different locations of site in science and design (Victoria Marshall 2003).

are color-coded **red** for science and **green** for design (Figure 4). In between these sections, portfolios of student work occupy the space of creative exploration and projection. We assembled four linking "threads of thought" to document this conversation and to offer another non-linear way to leaf through this book. Each section of student work is introduced by a different thread, and the threads are assembled to form sets of images that existed prior to the studio work, and others created during that time. The process of assembling offered clear as well as unexpected relationships. The thread diagrams are ordered according to those epiphanies of emerging knowledge, connection and juxtaposition. The relationship of the four threads to the composite image on pages 136-137 is that of finding a compelling and memorable image. The four threads are: Locating Models (pages 34-35), Landscape Loops (pages 58-59), Light Networks (pages 82-83), and Spiral Boundaries (pages 108-109). Each thread has key words and images that are mentioned in the text and threads of other chapters, providing alternative ways to leaf through this book.

Acknowledgements

The student work occupies the most challenging transdisciplinary space - between fields and discourses - and was guided by a diverse group of professionals. The five studios represented in this publication were coordinated by Urban Design Studio 2 Coordinator, Brian McGrath. In 2002, Adjunct Assistant Professor Victoria Marshall was the primary critic for Urban Design students' work, and Richard Plunz, Director of the Urban Design Program, taught a studio of graduate Architecture students. Marshall, McGrath, and Joel Towers co-taught three urban design studios during the Fall Semester of 2003. Dean Bernard Tschumi supported this studio with travel and publication funds in 2002, and Dean Mark Wigley has continued to support this collaboration since 2003. Richard Plunz, Director of the Urban Design Program, fully supported this work from its inception.

The work here has also benefited from the deep commitment of Drs. Steward T.A. Pickett and Mary L. Cadenasso from the Institute of Ecosystem Studies, Dr. J. Morgan Grove and Erika Svendsen from the USDA Forest Service, and Jackie Carrera and Guy Hager from Baltimore's Parks and People Foundation. Karen Hock carefully edited this book making the voices of many authors and disciplines coherent. Alanna Talty and Phanat Sonemangkhala patiently took the graphic design template prepared by Honest Design and made this book a reality. Additionally, we would like to thank the many people who gave their time, advice, and criticism in reviewing student presentations. Lastly and most importantly, we would like to recognize our students, who deserve much of the credit for the work and ideas contained here.

References

Appadurai, Arjun. 1996. Modernity at Large. Minneapolis: University of Minnesota Press.

Berger, John. 1972. Ways of Seeing. New York: Viking Press.

Castells, Manuel. 1999. The Culture of Cites in the Information Age. Available from: http://www.arch.columbia.edu/Buell/mmarchive/s_2001/castells/castells_fs.html

Genosko, Gary. 2002. Felix Guattari: Towards a Transdisciplinary Metamethodology. Angelaki 8: 1.

Harvey, David. 2000. Spaces of Hope. Berkeley: University of California Press.

Krauss, Rosalind. 1983. Sculpture in the Expanded Field. The Anti-Aesthetic: Essays on Postmodern Culture. Seattle: BayPress.

Mac, M.J., P.A. Opler, C.E. Puckett Haeker, and P.D. Doran. 1998. Status and Trends of the Nation's Biological Resources. United States Geological Survey. Available from: http://biology.usgs.gov/s+t/SNT/noframe/zy198.htm

Pickett, S.T.A. Baltimore Ecosystem Study, Long-Term Ecological Research Project Frequently Asked Questions: How is a city an ecosystem? Why is this research so novel? Available from: http://www.beslter.org/frame2-page_1_3.html

Van der Leeuw, Sander E. and Chr. Aschan-Leygonie. May 22-26, 2000. System Shocks-System Resilience. A Long-Term Perspective On Resilience In Socio-Natural Systems. Abisko, Sweden.

Thread A: Locating Models

This image diagram is a locality map of one of the core scientific frameworks we have been working with: the Human Ecosystem Framework (HEF). Starting with the HEF diagram on the far right, it splits into two; the link above provides an analogous description of our students' lived experience and creative projection from inside the framework. The link below looks at the framework from afar. It specifically targets the arrows, representing flows, that hold the framework together. In order to see these two links in relation to one another, the place of the questions that drive both ecology and design is mapped. Both fields use models, however the location of modeling varies between the fields (see figure 5, Chapter 1). From this new diagram, one student project on the far left leads the way forward into our collective work of critical reorganization of the questions asked of science and design (See larger image on pages 34-35).

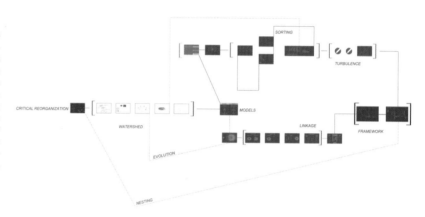

Thread A Diagram

Thread B: Landscape Loops

This image diagram engages the concepts used for understanding human systems in ecology and social science. Roughly ordered, the cycles of images are; time, information, networks and matter and around again. Although change is constant, patterns allow us to find legibility, and this provides a place to work. This image set can be read starting at any point, this allows each revisiting of an image to be re-read through the filter of new knowledge gained in the last pass, therefore revealing an individual pattern of understanding (See larger image on pages 58-59).

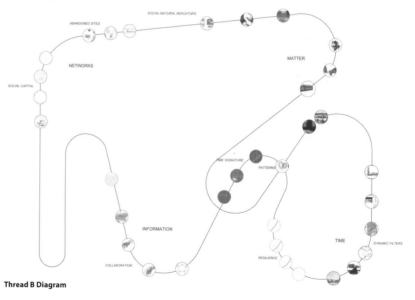

Thread B Diagram

Thread C: Light Networks

Drifting up and down scale and in and out of technologies, this image diagram is a search for two tools, first are those that don't reduce the complexity of the world into discrete abstract concepts and second a meditation on drawing, specifically the question: Is it possible to learn how systems work in real time through drawing?

This image diagram can be read as both a spectrum of juxtapositions or as a matrix across research and projects. As a matrix it could be understood a starter guide for urban design models that strive toward the goal of creating meaning. As shown in the diagram of meaning, model and metaphor (Pickett and Cadenasso 2002), when the image, method, theory and practice of a project all translate using one model, it has the potential to be a very powerful tool in mediating change (See larger image on pages 82-83).

Thread C Diagram

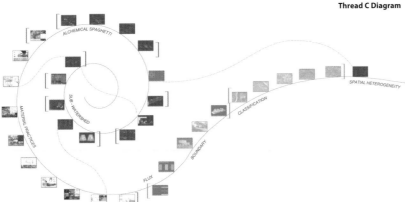

Thread D: Spiral Boundaries

Recent developments in the field of ecology use spatial heterogeneity as a significant concept. Translating this to urban design inherently repositions the radial model of the city separated by rural hinterland with a more patchy landscape that changes in time. The core organizing concept for this contemporary work is that of boundaries and flux, as it is the boundary of a system that change or flux across heterogeneous space can be measured and comparisons made. This image diagram is a tracking of a translation of spatial heterogeneities to urban design over the past two years. It is arranged in a spiral as it affords legibility of how the knowledge and memory of each project has influenced and informed the rest. Consistent is the understanding of the four-dimensional quality of boundaries and city models (See larger image on pages 108-109).

Thread D Diagram

CHAPTER I

MEANING, MODEL, AND METAPHOR OF PATCH DYNAMICS

DRS. S.T.A. PICKETT AND M.L. CADENASSO

Patch dynamics' primary utility for linking ecology and design in order to accomplish planning is as a provocative metaphor that practitioners from both disciplines find compelling. How does this metaphorical use relate to other ways it is used in science, and what does understanding the dimensions of patch dynamics as a concept tell us about how it might be rigorously used in design and planning? How should urban designers use a patch dynamics approach?

Like all scientific concepts, patch dynamics has three components: a core meaning or definition, a suite of ways to specify the concept in particular models or applications, and the already-mentioned metaphorical dimension. The metaphorical connotation of any scientific concept allows the idea to be communicated to the public, to specialists in other disciplines, and even to schools of ecology beyond those which generally use it.

We can exhibit this multidimensionality of concepts by using another well known ecological idea, the ecosystem (Pickett and Cadenasso 2002). We use the ecosystem concept here both because it provides a well-developed example of the dimensionality of ecological concepts, and because it is useful in translating patch dynamics to urban design. At its core, the **meaning** of "ecosystem" is a specified area of the Earth, in which biological components and the physical environment interact with one another. This general definition is specified—or turned into a **model**—to apply to certain situations and collections of organisms found in particular places. For example, there is the model of ecosystem function at the Hubbard Brook Experimental Forest in New Hampshire, which allowed the discovery of acid rain in North America. The ecosystems at Hubbard Brook are defined by small watersheds, and are limited underground by a nearly impervious bedrock (Likens and Bormann 1995). The study of nutrients and chemistry of the streams draining each spatially delimited watershed was key to discovering acid rain and learning how it affected ecosystems (Likens 1992). The third dimension of the ecosystem concept, the **metaphor**, is used in informal or non-specialized communication. People often use the term ecosystem to refer to an area of the world they are interested in simply to identify it as a place, or perhaps more provocatively to assume something about how the biological processes in the area work. The metaphorical dimension of the ecosystem concept is often used to connote self-regulation, or a closed network of energy and matter flow (Golley 1993). Using such metaphors of the ecosystem expresses values in the public discourse about environmental policy, for example. We will use the ecosystem concept when we translate patch dynamics to the design realm (Figure 5).

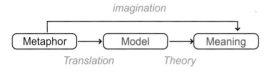

Figure 5. Meaning, model and metaphor (S. T. A. Pickett 2002).

Patch Dynamics as Metaphor

We see that all ecological concepts will have a core definition, will need to be applied through specific models, and will have informal, imagistic content as metaphors. How does patch dynamics fit this mold? First, its metaphorical connotations are images of spatial heterogeneity, or patchiness in the environment. The term itself suggests images of patchwork quilts, or mosaics of different colors and patterns of fabric stitched together to form the familiar coverlets of folk origin. The term also suggests complex configurations of the elements of a pattern, similar to Byzantine mosaics composed of hundreds of individual tiles. Lastly, patch dynamics metaphorically invokes a sense of ongoing change, perhaps something like the shifting patterns of a kaleidoscope. These images are useful in initiating a scientific concept, or in communicating it in vernacular conversation. But they are not adequate for rigorous quantitative comparison, experimental manipulation, and interdisciplinary synthesis. For this, other dimensions of the concept are required.

Defining Patch Dynamics

The first step toward scientific rigor is a technical definition that captures the insights of the metaphor (Pickett and White 1985). Patch dynamics is defined through three components. First is the existence of patches—on land or in aquatic systems—that differ from one another in species composition,

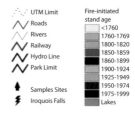

		Fire-initiated
	UTM Limit	stand age

UTM Limit
Roads
Rivers
Railway
Hydro Line
Park Limit

Samples Sites
Iroquois Falls

Fire-initiated
stand age
<1760
1760-1769
1800-1820
1850-1859
1860-1899
1900-1924
1925-1949
1950-1974
1975-1999
Lakes

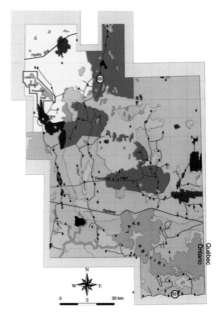

Figure 6. Map of time since fire within the Lake Abitibi Model Forest, Ontario and Quebec, Canada. By taking cores in old trees, ecologists and foresters are able to map the extent of fires of different ages. Younger fires have consumed some of the area that had belonged to older fires. Over time, the mosaic changes as new fires burn the area. The vegetation structure changes in burned patches through time as a result of succession. The combination of fires of different ages, new fires, and the succession in patches after fires leads to a very dynamic landscape, of which the map here is merely a snap shot. Maps such as this represent a simple patch dynamics model. (Prepared by Dr. Sylvie Gaultier. Used by permission of Natural Resources Canada, Canadian Forest Service, Laurentian Forestry Centre, from Information Report LAU-X-125.)

physical structure, or ecological processes. The second component of the definition is the fact that individual patches change through time, as a result of succession, or as a consequence of the movement of materials, energy, and organisms among them. Third, if individual patches change, then so too will the entire array of patches. Bormann and Likens (1979) use a related metaphor to capture the images encapsulated in this three-part definition: the shifting mosaic. Of course, not only does the arrangement of the "mosaic tiles" shift in ecological mosaics, but also their size and color. The relationship of the definition and the metaphor show the limitations of each, and the power of the pairing.

Patch Dynamics Models

Patch dynamics as a general concept alone has little power to advance ecological science. The advance comes in the application of the general concept in specific models. Models are the tools that put meanings into practice. In the case of patch dynamics, models can exactly quantify patches, assess the processes that occur within patches, determine the fluxes that link them, and identify the boundaries that govern the fluxes. A pioneering example of a patch dynamic model is the characterization of the fire dynamics of the boreal coniferous forests of the Boundary Waters Canoe Area in Minnesota (Heinselman 1973). This model had as a key component the form of a seemingly simple map, but it was groundbreaking at the time it was introduced. It depicted how long ago each area of the region experienced a fire that destroyed the forest canopy and allowed new trees to establish. Such maps are the first step in illustrating the extremely dynamic nature of this large landscape, and show that all areas had burned at some time in the past, resulting in a mosaic of forest stands of different ages. Figure 6 shows a similar map for the Lake Abitibi Model Forest in Quebec. Other contemporary patch dynamics models take maps of disturbance and succession in the different patches and go on to characterize the nutrient processes in each patch type. Such models have been constructed for Yellowstone National Park, for example, where animal populations interact with plants of different species and nutrient status in the contrasting array of patches (Turner and others 1994). These contemporary patch models show the many layers of interacting processes that are involved in shifting mosaic landscapes.

One important feature of the concept of patch dynamics, like many other important ecological concepts, is that it can apply to many different kinds of systems and spatial and temporal scales. It is not necessary to apply the term only to large landscapes like the Boundary Waters, or Yellowstone National Park. Rather, it can also be used to examine fine-scale shifts in spatial heterogeneity, such as the migrating patches of clonal plants in a meadow. Another fine-scale example is the creation of pits and associated mounds by porcupines along a few meters of hillside in a small desert watershed. These pits and mounds appear and disappear across the desert as porcupines dig for bulbs of perennial plants. After the porcupine moves on, the pits fill and the mounds erode. Patch dynamics has even been applied productively to streams (Fisher 1998).

A Framework for Patch Dynamics

Part of the way that ecologists specify or translate their general concepts into useful, specific models is to employ frameworks (Cadenasso and others 2003). Frameworks link general concepts to specific tools. A causal framework is a conceptual structure that enumerates and links the important causes and factors that affect a phenomenon or process of interest. Causal frameworks provide a complete roster of the causes that can explain the phenomenon, and they provide a hierarchical structure to relate general to specific causes. The hierarchical form indicates that the general causes are broken down into more specific causes that make them up. These features of frameworks suggest the content and level of generality of the quantitative models, the experiments, and the comparisons that ecologists use to study their subject matter. The general causes apply over large areas or averaged conditions, while the more specific, component causes refer to the precise conditions and interactions that occur at particular locations and times. When scientists build models, they select the components from the appropriate hierarchical level of their causal framework.

The patch dynamics framework takes as its focal phenomenon the alteration of structure and function of spatial heterogeneity over time. This statement describes the highest hierarchical level of the framework, and comprises four more specific processes: 1) mosaic configuration, 2) patch generation, 3) patch change, and 4) flux among patches (Figure 7).

Mosaic configuration means, first, that the heterogeneity of an area can be delineated as patches, and that those patches have a spatially explicit relationship to one another (Figure 8). Patch delineation requires that areas differ from one another in structure, composition, or function. Spatially explicit relationships are revealed by maps, volumetric models, or by distance measures that show the spatial relationship of each patch to every other patch in the array. In this way, functions or changes in any one patch can be related to processes or patterns in neighboring patches. Spatially explicit models are required to evaluate the effects of neighborhood or adjacency of patches. Patch mosaics and volumes can exist on any spatial or temporal scale, and these must be defined by the researcher.

Patch generation refers to all processes that can create new patches in an area. In ecology, they can be physical forces that destroy existing vegetation cover, or generative biological processes that build new structures (Pickett and others 2000). We therefore group patch-forming processes into those that are disturbances and those that are the engineering effects of organisms. Any ecologically relevant process can generate patchiness if it acts differentially and locally across an extensive surface or volume.

Patch change can be caused by numerous factors. Perhaps the most familiar ecological process of patch change is succession, the change in species composition or architecture of an assemblage of organisms at a site over time. Succession in turn has many causes, ranging from competition to dispersal to physiological tolerances to the effects of animal consumers on

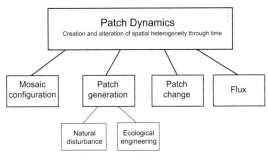

Figure 7. A causal framework for patch dynamics. The highest level of the framework identifies the phenomenon of interest as the creation and alteration of spatial heterogeneity of ecological systems through time. The next level identifies the major causes of patch dynamics as mosaic configuration, patch generation, patch change, and the fluxes that connect and affect patches. Although each of the second level causes can be further subdivided into additional, detailed causes, we only illustrate that division for patch generation. Patch generation is caused either by natural disturbances or by the engineering effects of physical or biological factors.

Figure 8. An ecological patch mosaic at the medium scale. This slope in the Negev Desert, Israel, can be conceived of as consisting of two contrasting kinds of patches: rock and soil. These two patch types differ in their role in the water dynamics of the system, with rocky patches shedding runoff water, and soil patches absorbing it. The soil patches come to have more water available than they would based on rainfall alone, and support diverse communities of annuals and bulb-bearing perennials. Herbivorous animals in turn find high levels of resources available in the soil patches.

the plant community. However, to understand patch dynamics, it is sufficient to recognize that succession can act to change the nature of patches in mosaics. Patch change by succession focuses attention on within-patch processes. However, patch change can also be generated by fluxes of important ecological agents from outside individual patches. Patch change can be caused by the movement of organisms or the flux of nutrients or pollutants across mosaics (Cadenasso and others 2003). Any material, energy, or information that can cause local ecological responses, and which moves or is effective differentially across an area, can act to cause changes in sensitive patches.

As expected from the definition of a causal framework stated earlier, the general process of patch change is made up of other, more specific mechanisms or causes. We have already mentioned that patch generation can have the component processes of either disturbance or ecological engineering. In the same way, mosaic configuration may reflect underlying geological or climatic templates. Similarly, the detailed processes of succession - which are differential site availability, differential species availability, and differential species performance - are the subsidiary mechanisms of patch change and are shown in Figure 9 (Pickett and others 1987).

Fluxes among patches are governed by processes including patch contrast, the

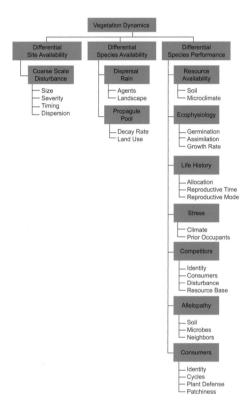

Figure 9. A causal framework for community succession or vegetation dynamics. At the top of the hierarchy, the phenomenon of interest is identified. Community dynamics is defined as the change in species composition and three dimensional structure over time. Three subsidiary causes result in the general phenomenon of vegetation dynamics: differential site availability, differential species availability, and differential species performance. In turn, each of the subsidiary causes is made up of additional factors that influence it. General explanations of succession reside at the high levels of cause, while very specific, detailed models that apply to specific sites and periods of time incorporate the detailed factors that underlie the subsidiary causes (Modified from Pickett et al 1987).

nature of the flux, and the nature of the boundaries between patches. These components themselves constitute a boundary framework which is important for design (Cadenasso and others 2003). This framework and its implications will be detailed in Chapter V, *Boundaries as Structural and Functional Entities in Landscapes: Understanding Flows in Ecology and Urban Design.*

Frameworks Are Not the Same as Theories

Rather, frameworks are a part of theory. Theory consists of many more components, such as definitions, assumptions, generalizations, and models (Pickett and others 1994). Enumerating and characterizing all the components of patch dynamics theory and specifying how they are linked to the general framework is beyond the scope of this chapter. Here we emphasize that patch models translate the general features of patch dynamics included in the framework into specific representations of patch structure and change.

We expect the general framework of patch dynamics to be able to change to reflect new information or new tests of hypotheses about patch dynamics. Patch dynamics is such a fundamental way to address spatial heterogeneity that we would be surprised if new and perhaps seemingly contradictory observations couldn't ultimately be accommodated by identifying new relationships or incorporating new processes into the framework. What does get thrown out or altered at a rapid rate are the models or hypotheses that apply to very specific situations and relationships. If one considers the framework to be a tree, with the trunk representing the core process, and the major limbs representing the primary contributing causes, then the smaller twigs and leaves represent the models and hypotheses that are proposed, tested, and replaced or refined very rapidly (Figure 10). Just as deciduous trees lose and replace their leaves in response to drought, so too do frameworks elaborate and replace specific models and hypotheses depending on the success of experimental and observational tests. In other words, the stress of experiment or mismatch with observation kills off certain leaves and twigs

Figure 10. A baobab tree. Like many trees in arid environments, baobabs lose leaves in drought periods. They may also lose twigs in especially dry periods, and if large branches are damaged by animals, they may also be lost. However, during favorable periods leaves are produced again, and new branches are even produced. Hence, this tree is a metaphor for robust conceptual frameworks in science. Leaves and twigs are produced to capture light and the gain is invested in maintenance and in the durable woody structure. Leaves and twigs are, however, disposable entities, and if they encounter an unfavorable environment, they are shed to protect the tree as a whole. Models, tests, and experiments are the "organs" that theories produce to probe the envelope of understanding. If the models don't prove to be correct, or if the experiments fail, it turns out that most often it is the models and experiments that are faulty, not the large trunk of a well developed and robust theory.

that aren't well adapted. The intermediate sized branches stand for model types that have proven to be robust or generalizable in the topic area. Medium sized branches also stand for empirical generalizations about the way patch dynamics works that have withstood repeated tests. The key idea is that sometimes models are incorrect and must be completely thrown out, and sometimes defective models can be improved. Often the learning that results from model rejection or improvement shows some factor or relationship that had previously been left out of a framework. Thus, the cycle of learning by building, testing, and correcting models can expand or strengthen the frameworks they represent.

Applying Patch Dynamics to Human Ecosystems

Patch dynamics was developed in biological ecology, and the examples and structures we have presented above reflect that origin. If we are to succeed in our proposition that patch dynamics might motivate urban designers, and that this motivation may proceed beyond the merely metaphorical, then we must link the bioecological concept with the phenomena of human ecosystems. We presented the ecological concept of ecosystem earlier. Now we are in a position to ask, how do the ideas of mosaic configuration, patch generation, patch change, and cross-patch flux apply to urban ecosystems? The human ecosystem framework (Figure 11) provides for social functions, the cycles or dynamics of change, and the processes which order social and institutional relationships. All of these phenomena can act on the ecological and social resources of the resource system. Specific models of processes and dynamics in urban systems would draw on the human ecosystem framework to select causes from the biological and socio-economic realms to tie together as multidimensional causes and results of interactions in these complex, coupled biological-social systems.

Are urban systems patchy, and can the models using the integrated processes suggested by the human ecosystem framework be applied to urban patch dynamics? We believe they can. Urban systems, which include in the broadest sense suburban areas and the exurban fringe, are notoriously patchy. In Figure 12, an area of Baltimore illustrates the point. Using a new high categorical resolution classification developed by M.L. Cadenasso, some 90 possible categories of urban patches based jointly on built structures, the aggregation of paved areas, and vegetation can be identified. The preliminary classification of this area shows just how patchy cities can be. This application of patch dynamics will be all the more appropriate if causes of patch generation, causes of patch change, and causes of flux across patches include processes suggested by the human ecosystem framework as well as the traditional processes of ecology. Combining the ecological framework of patch dynamics and the interdisciplinary human ecosystem framework indicates how appropriate the application of patch dynamics is to urban systems.

There is an important change in the general set of background assumptions—the paradigm of ecology—that has informed patch dynamics, and so should inform its application in design. In the past, ecologists considered the systems they studied to have six key features. First, they were assumed to be materially closed. This means that most of the material exchanges that were thought to be important took place within the system. This assumption led to the second—that ecological systems were self regulating. In other words, the interactions and limits that governed the behavior, growth, or persistence of ecological systems

Human Ecological System

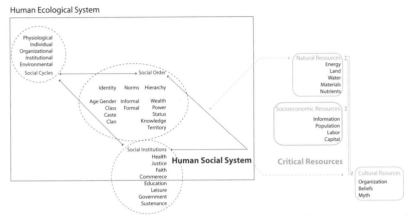

Figure 11. The human ecosystem framework. This hierarchical, causal structure suggests the component structures and processes that make up inhabited, built, or managed ecosystems. Of course, such systems have essential biological components that are the foundational resources, but they also reflect social and cultural resources, and possess a social system through which human individuals and various aggregations of people interact and are organized (Based on the work of Machlis et al 1997).

Figure 12. A patch mosaic from Baltimore, Maryland. Based on a novel classification by M.L. Cadenasso and others, this preliminary patch mosaic was created for an area centered on the Rognel Heights neighborhood. The classification emphasizes both the built and the natural components of the environment, being based on three dimensions of building type and density, vegetation type and layering, and the presence of massed parking areas. The heterogeneity illustrated by this example is typical of urban areas.

could be found within them. Third, ecological systems were considered to have stable equilibrium points, meaning that they would have a single, specific composition or behavior that was stable and persistent. This opened the way to the fourth assumption, that ecological systems were rarely disturbed. If disturbance did occur in an ecological system, it was then assumed to undergo a predictable sequence of stages to recover its temporarily lost equilibrium. In other words, when disturbed, systems would exhibit predictable, directional successions or recovery dynamics. Finally, ecological systems were classically assumed not to include humans. Ecologists looked far and wide to find systems to study that were apparently unaffected by humans.

These six background assumptions were very rarely articulated in ecology, yet they guided how ecologists built models, what kinds of systems they studied, and the kinds of processes and interactions they included in those studies and models. However, as data on system behavior over long periods of time accumulated, and as observations could span broader and broader scales due to the growing data bases in many places or due to remote sensing, ecologists discovered that their background assumptions were not always correct. As a result, over the last ten or twelve years, ecologists have articulated a new paradigm that better fits the facts as they are now known. This paradigm is sometimes called the non-equilibrium paradigm because it does not assume that the equilibrium seeking or maintaining behaviors that were emphasized in the classical paradigm are the dominant force in ecology (Pickett and others 1992). Ecologists now recognize the following:

1. Ecological systems can be open to material exchange with other systems.

2. Factors from outside a specified system can regulate system behavior.

3. There may not be a single stable equilibrium point for system composition or behavior.

4. Disturbance can be a part of the dynamics of a system .

5. Succession or response to disturbance can be highly unpredictable or probabilistic.

6. Humans, including their institutions and behaviors, can be parts of ecological systems.

It is in the context of the new, non-equilibrium paradigm that patch dynamics must be seen. Patch dynamics is a framework and modeling strategy that takes into account the spatial openness and context of ecological systems. It emphasizes their ability to change and to respond to internal and external forces. It is one of the important mechanisms for the resilience or adaptability of all sorts of ecological systems. In other words, patch dynamics is one of the key ways that ecologists can see how the non-equilibrium paradigm applies to many ecological systems.

Linking Patch Dynamics with Urban Design

Patch dynamics in ecology has been presented as a core concept, a framework showing how to generate specific models, and a metaphor that reflects the core concept in imagistic terms (Pickett and others 2004). It also calls to mind the points of the contemporary, non-equilibrium paradigm.

What of this apparatus do we expect to be useful in urban design? Do we expect the patch dynamics models of ecology to translate to urban design? No. Ecological models appropriately deal with the way that ecologists measure mosaic configuration, or detect and study patch generation and change, or evaluate the role of flux across mosaics of patches. Some of this may be directly relevant to design when it focuses on the green infrastructure of cities. And when it does so, it should be applied. Indeed, models of urban green patch dynamics are urgently needed to help inform management of parks and green spaces, as discussed in Chapter III (Flores and others 1997).

However, the patch dynamics of the bulk of the metropolis will require integrated models that explicitly incorporate the structures and processes contained in the human ecosystem framework. Such models are still in their formative stage, but have much promise for the future. The application of patch dynamics to design problems requires still further steps. Either the human ecosystem framework can be modified to specify how design considerations should be included in patch dynamics models, or a design-specific framework can be invented.

Perhaps the most approachable way to link patch dynamics with design processes is to start with designs as models or designs as parts of more extensive urban patch dynamics. In fact, designs are working or hypothetical models of an urban ecological system, or of a small part of an urban ecosystem. If that design has explicitly incorporated and articulated the concerns of the human ecosystem framework along with an explicit statement of the constraints and drivers of design, then it becomes a model in the same way that ecological propositions and experiments are models. In fact, we can restate the patch dynamics framework in terms of urban design (Figure 13). In a patch dynamics/design framework, the most general process—now seen as a goal—is the design of urban spatial heterogeneity. The component processes would be the spatial configuration of designed spaces, the modes of creation of designed spaces, the change in designed spaces, and the fluxes that designed spaces participate in, control, and are

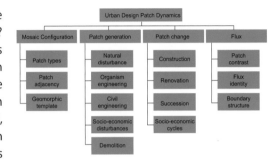

Figure 13. A framework for designed patch dynamics. This is an exploratory effort to cast the process of urban design in a framework that parallels that for patch dynamics that has been developed in ecology. Patch mosaics in the urban context will include natural vegetation, streams, lakes, and substrate based patches, as well as "vacant" lands abandoned or not yet developed, infrastructure, landscaped and managed lands, and various kinds of buildings and structures that are the direct product and concern of designers. The social, economic, and cultural causes represented in the Human Ecosystem Framework will have to be accounted for among the lower levels of the causal hierarchy. This hierarchy is presented as a skeleton to promote integration and dialogue with designers, not as a complete conceptual construct.

Discipline	Paradigm	
	Equilibrium	Non-Equilibrium
Ecology	Ecosystems in balance	Ecosystem resilience
Landscape	Static landscapes	Dynamic landscapes
Architecture	Sustainable Design	Avant Garde Design
Urban Design	Normative models	Designed models of patch dynamics

Table 1. An illustrative and speculative relationship between key ideas associated with the equilibrium versus non-equilibrium paradigm in ecology and in urban design. We purposefully leave the cell relating the non-equilibrium paradigm to design principles blank, as a stimulus to dialogue with ecologically motivated urban designers.

controlled by. Because designed spaces are parts of human ecosystems, the components of the human ecosystem framework would suggest the subsidiary causes that make up each of the primary component processes.

Designs, as models operationalizing the general patch dynamics/design framework, can serve as vehicles to test the assumptions and processes of patch dynamics in the realm of built spaces (Pickett and others 2004). Ecologically informed designs could also help bring the seemingly abstract principles of the non-equilibrium paradigm of ecology into the urban context (Table 1). The job falls to designers working with the patch dynamics framework themselves, or to interdisciplinary teams of designers and ecologists working together not only to provide interesting and viable designs, but to elaborate designs as parts of patch dynamics models.

Conclusion

Designs as models of patch dynamics, where such models serve the needs of clients and the public and incorporate the best creativity and analysis that designers are capable of, can serve both design and ecology. Ecology in the urban context has two concerns. The first is to extend its own explanatory scope. This means making sure that ecology can explain and understand the patterns and processes in the coupled human/ "natural" systems of cities, suburbs, and the exurban fringe. But it also means assuring that concerns of biological and social resilience are met in urban ecosystems. Patch dynamics has a role to play in both of these concerns. For too long, ecologists have seen cities as a foreign land and have neglected to bring their best ideas to them. We hope that patch dynamics can survive as an ecological concept when translated into this new realm. But we also hope that patch dynamics may support designers in their desire to repair and expose the ecological processes in cities (Thompson and Steiner 1997). to design in ways that are resilient to ecological, social, and economic changes, and to see their designs as ecological systems or parts of ecological systems. The new, non-equilibrium paradigm of ecology can help support this application as well. Here it is important to recognize a developing concept of ecological resilience that accounts for the ability of systems to adjust and adapt, rather than merely return to a fixed reference point after disruption (Gunderson and others 1995). The models of designers—designs and plans themselves— become the models that apply the patch dynamics framework, leavened by the concepts and processes of the human ecosystem framework, to cities, towns, neighborhoods, and the urban-rural fringe. If this can be achieved, the potential of the metaphor of patch dynamics will have been converted to a rigorous tool for integrating ecology and design.

References

Bormann, F. H., and G. E. Likens. 1979. Catastrophic Disturbance and the Steady-State in Northern Hardwood Forests. American Scientist 67: 660-669.

Cadenasso, M.L., S.T.A. Pickett, K.C. Weathers, and C.G. Jones. 2003. A Framework for a Theory of Ecological Boundaries. BioScience 53: 750-758.

Fisher, S. 1998. Hierarchy, Spatial Configuration, and Nutrient Cycling in a Desert Stream. Australian Journal of Ecology 23 : 41-52.

Flores, A., S.T.A. Pickett, W.C. Zipperer, R.V. Pouyat, and R. Pirani. 1997. Adopting a modern Modern Ecological View of the Metropolitan Landscape: The Case of a Greenspace System for the New York City Region. Landscape and Urban Planning 39: 295-308.

Golley, F.B. 1993. A History of the Ecosystem Concept in Ecology: More Than the Sum of the Parts. New Haven: Yale University Press.

Gunderson, L.H., C.S. Holling, and S.S. Light, editors. 1995. Barriers and Bridges to the Renewal of Ecosystems and Institutions. New York: Columbia University Press.

Heinselman, M.L. 1973. Fire in the Virgin Forests of the Boundary Waters Canoe Area, Minnesota. Journal of Quaternary Research 3: 329-382.

Likens, G.E. 1992. The Ecosystem Approach: Its Use and Abuse. Oldendorf/Luhe, Germany: Ecology Institute.

Likens, G.E., and F.H. Bormann. 1995. Biogeochemistry of a Forested Ecosystem. New York: Springer-Verlag.

Machlis, G.E., J.E. Force, and W.R. Burch. 1997. The Human Ecosystem, 1. The Human Ecosystem as an Organizing Concept in Ecosystem Management. Society and Natural Resources 10: 347-367.

Pickett, S.T.A., and M.L. Cadenasso. 2002. Ecosystem as a Multidimensional Concept: Meaning, Model and Metaphor. Ecosystems 5: 1-10.

Pickett, S.T.A., M.L. Cadenasso, and C.G. Jones. 2000. Generation of Heterogeneity by Organisms: Creation, Maintenance, and Transformation. In Hutchings, M., editor. Ecological Consequences of Habitat Heterogeneity. New York: Blackwell. pp. 33-52.

Pickett, S.T.A., S.L. Collins, and J.J. Armesto. 1987. Models, Mechanisms and Pathways of Succession. Botanical Review 53: 335-371.

Pickett, S.T.A., J. Kolasa, and C.G. Jones. 1994. Ecological Understanding: The Nature of Theory and the Theory of Nature. San Diego: Academic Press.

Pickett, S.T.A., and P.S. White. 1985. Patch Dynamics: a Synthesis. Pages 371-384 in S.T.A. Pickett, editor. The Ecology of Natural Disturbance and Patch Dynamics. Orlando: Academic Press.

Pickett, S.T.A., M.L. Cadenasso, and J.M. Grove. 2004. Resilient Cities: Meaning, Models, and Metaphor for integrating Integrating the Ecological, Socio-economic, and Planning Realms. Landscape and Urban Planning. In press.

Thompson, G.F., and C.F. Steiner, editors. 1997. Ecological Design and Planning. New York: John Wiley and Sons.

Turner, M.G., Y. Wu, L.L. Wallace, and W.H. Romme. 1994. Simulating Winter Interactions Among Ungulates, Vegetation, and Fire in Northern Yellowstone Park. Ecological Applications 4: 472-496.

THREAD A:
LOCATING FRAMEWORKS

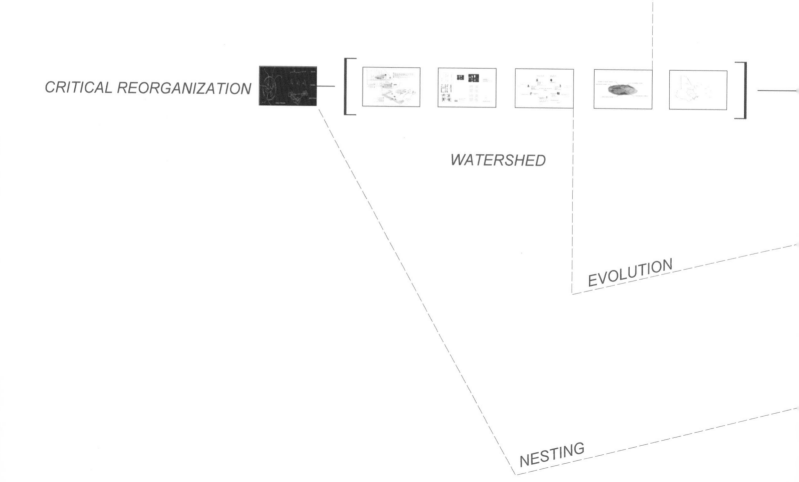

CRITICAL REORGANIZATION

WATERSHED

EVOLUTION

NESTING

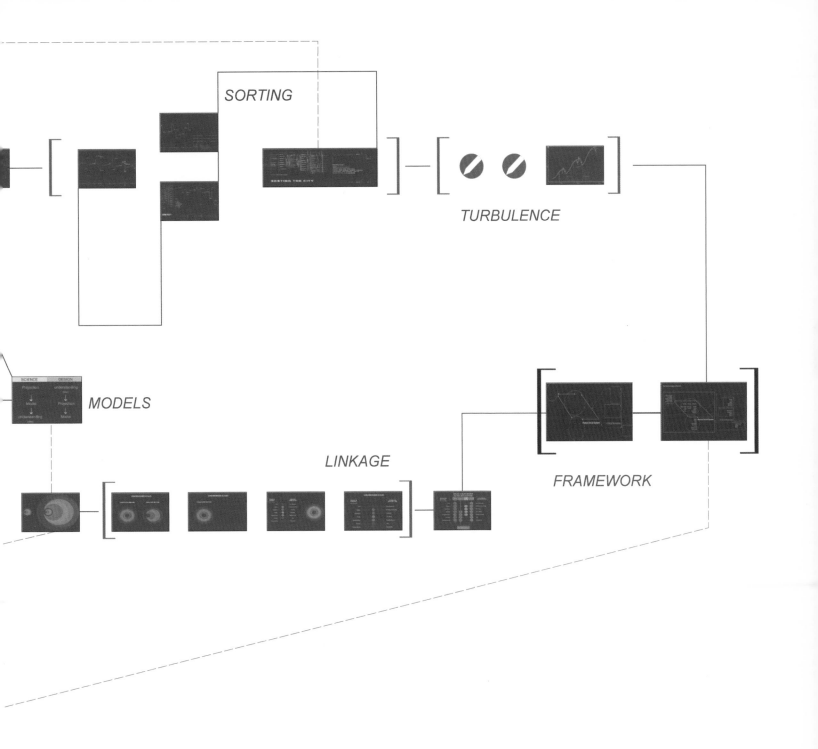

SORTING

TURBULENCE

MODELS

LINKAGE

FRAMEWORK

SYNCHRONIZED SCALES

CLOSED-LOOP NESTING   OPEN-LOOP NESTING

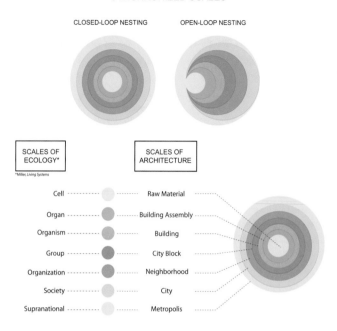

SCALES OF ECOLOGY*
*Miller, Living Systems

SCALES OF ARCHITECTURE

Scales of Ecology	Scales of Architecture
Cell	Raw Material
Organ	Building Assembly
Organism	Building
Group	City Block
Organization	Neighborhood
Society	City
Supranational	Metropolis

Synchronized Scales
Petia Morozov, 2003

While it may be difficult to identify where the edge of one scale ends and another begins, this coordination of scales synchronizes architecture with ecology at a fundamental level. For the purposes of the translation, the actual categorization is less important than the realization that every system impacts others in critical ways.

-Petia Morozov. 2003. Urban Legends Symposium.

The workings of evolution are clearest at the level of genes and individuals and become fuzzier as we move up the chain of organization to groups and populations, to interactions between species, and ultimately to ecosystems and the biosphere. Indeed my central thesis has been that ecosystem structure and dynamics emerge from selection operating at lower levels, and that feedbacks from higher levels are weak because of individualistic distribution of species.

-Simon Levin. 2000. 'Fragile Dominion: Complexity and the Commons.'

FIELDS-SCALES MATRIX
RELEVANT FIELDS OF INQUIRY

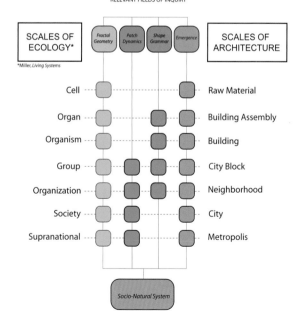

SCALES OF ECOLOGY*
*Miller, Living Systems

Fractal Geometry · Patch Dynamics · Shape Grammar · Emergence

SCALES OF ARCHITECTURE

Cell — Raw Material
Organ — Building Assembly
Organism — Building
Group — City Block
Organization — Neighborhood
Society — City
Supranational — Metropolis

Socio-Natural System

Fields Scale Matrix
Petia Morozov, 2003

"Taking a hierarchy of scale as a system of organization, this diagram makes spatial the contemporary fields of inquiry into human ecosystem dynamics. Inherent in this matrix is an interconnectedness of scales and the non-linearity of complex systems."
 We can reimagine architect Morozov's formulation by changing the word architecture in the diagram to "urban design" which could encompass the wider field of natural systems.

-Petia Morozov. 2003. Urban Legends Symposium.

Lifecourse: Micro-macro
Erika Svendsen, 2004

It is not surprising that urban field observations have suggested that community-based projects which are linked initially to a disturbance, trauma and/or loss are embedded with social meaning shaped by local identity, values and traditions but affected by regional networks and more global events. Projects which have the greatest potential to re-knit social cohesion are those which help re-establish a locus of control, neighborhood efficacy and collective resilience. Projects that are imbued with an ecological approach in process, design and maintenance have even higher potentials of fostering open systems essential for freedom of expression, building trust, creating social equity and improving public health. Taken as a whole, these projects are 'landscapes of resilience' and did not originate from a planner's map but emerge from a process of social reorganization.
In trying to draw, describe and understand these landscapes, we are challenged by several questions. How do we locate collective resilience? How do social networks connect at multiple scales? What are the core values which connect them? These questions are complicated by the fact that social ecologists, economists and epidemiologists have determined that systems are 'leaky' particularly at the stage of 'reorganization.' And we find that 'what is lost and what is gained' is either measured in a single time scale or filtered through limited narratives of power and legitimacy. Thus, for long-term research the challenge many not only be to gather information over time but how to measure time, particularly with relationship to collective memory and lagged effects.
Science which can inform the process of mediating change becomes essential to understanding our capacity for change. We must know what are the precise conditions under which human societies are willing to accept constraint and sacrifice. What are the conditions under which a civic responsibility will rise above consumptive preferences and property rights? What has social meaning? What is sacred? Who mediates what is lost and what is gained?

-Erika Svendsen. 2004. 'Landscapes of Resilience'. Unpublished.

Preliminary Mapping of Ideas
for Designed Urban Experiments
Alex Felson 2004

This diagram offers a medium through which ecologists and designers could communicate by sorting socio-natural processes along four poles defined by different human/natural relationships. By organizing the spatial, temporal, modular and geometric characteristics of ecological and design experiments in this way, the diagram allows ecologists and designers to develop physical projects for research purposes. In addition it proposes that these experimental designs become part of a large ecological and design lexicon for the selection of multiple tools, methods and sites of an experimental ecological design.

-Alex Felson. 2004. From seminar description: 'Ecology, Aesthetics and Representation' ; and Victoria Marshall

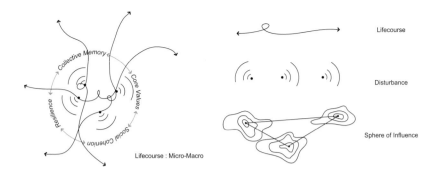

Lifecourse

Disturbance

Sphere of Influence

Lifecourse : Micro-Macro

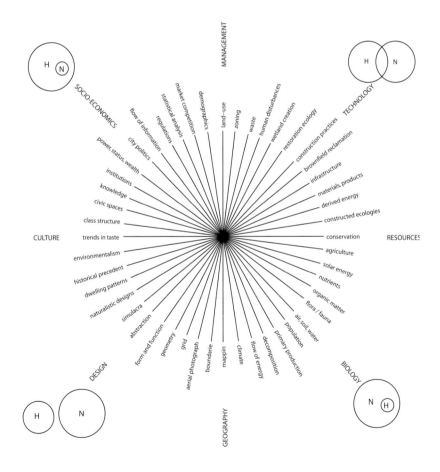

URBAN DESIGN STUDIO WORK 2002, GWYNNS FALLS WATERSHED.
Victoria Marshall, Critic. Marc Brossa, Yu-Heng Chiang, Kratma Saini,
Pavithra Sriprakash, John Tran, Students.

Sorting Diagram, Gwynns Falls
Renie Tang 2002

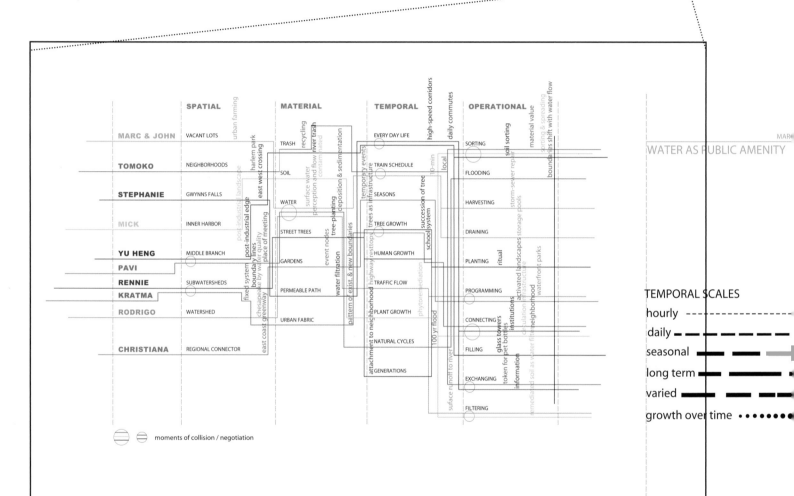

SORTING THE CITY

VACANT LOTS urban farming

WATER surface water

TRAIN SCHEDULE 10-min walk

HARVESTING storm-sewer repair storage pools

DRAINING

TERRITORY OF EXCHANGE

TOMOKO NEIGHBORHOODS harlem park TRASH recycling TR

VACANT LOTS   urban farming   WATER   surface water   TRAIN SCHEDULE   10-min walk   HARVESTING   storm-sewer repair storage pools   DRAINING   TOMOKO   NEIGHBORHOODS   harlem park   TRASH   recycling   TR

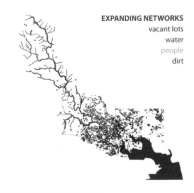

EXPANDING NETWORKS
vacant lots
water
people
dirt

EXPANDING NETWORKS
neighborhoods
water
forest cover

EXISTING

Alchemical Spaghetti: Networks
UD student collaborative model, 2002

Alchemical Spaghetti: Fields
UD student collaborative model, 2002

TRANSFORMED

Alchemical Spaghetti: Composite
UD student collaborative model, 2002

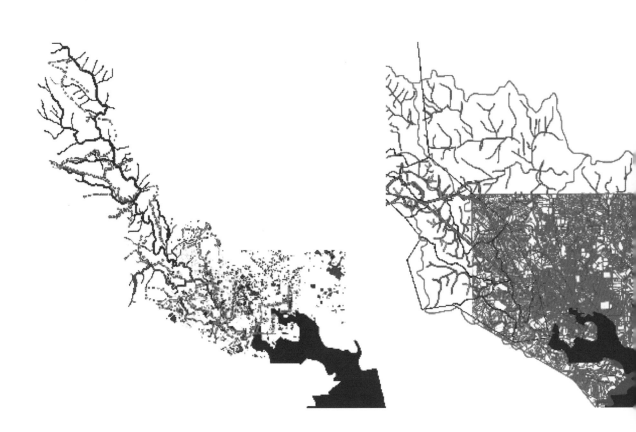

EXPANDING NETWORKS   FIELDS

EXPANDING NETWORKS
connection
water
neighborhoods
trail
people

Alchemical Spaghetti: Disturbance
UD student collaborative model, 2002

Deposition and Sedimentation Landscape
Yu-Heng Chiang, 2002

After making a study of the edge of the Middle Branch, I found distinct patterns of deposition and sedimentation in the postindustrial sites on the ground. The elevated high-speed corridors of roads and rail lines bypassed these. This is the landscape that the Gwyns Falls drains into and I was struck by the lack of dialogue between these three systems. *(continued next page)*

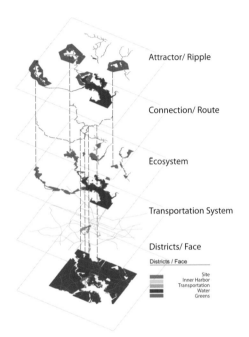

Attractor/ Ripple

Connection/ Route

Ecosystem

Transportation System

Districts/ Face

Districts / Face

Site
Inner Harbor
Transportation
Water
Greens

DISTURBANCE

Glass Sorting Towers
Yu-Heng Chiang, 2002

My project engages the high-speed system with a series of glass sorting towers. The spatial array of the towers marks this territory of crossing. Each tower is a measure of material that has been discarded and then collected into this downstream location. Periodically the towers are emptied and it is possible to see through them, past the stormwater outfalls, and up into the Gwynns Falls watershed.

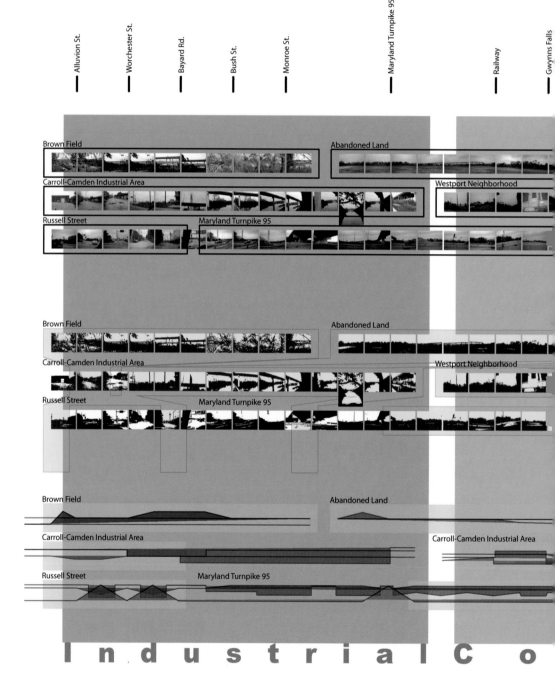

Water Front

Neighborhood Area

Highway

Out Loop

Mid Loop

Inner Loop

Water Access
View
Speed
View
Water Access
Speed
View
Speed
Water Access

Alluvion St.

Worchester St.

Bayard Rd.

Bush St.

Monroe St.

Maryland Turnpike 95

Railway

Gwynns Falls

Brown Field

Carroll-Camden Industrial Area

Russell Street

Maryland Turnpike 95

Abandoned Land

Westport Neighborhood

IndustrialCo

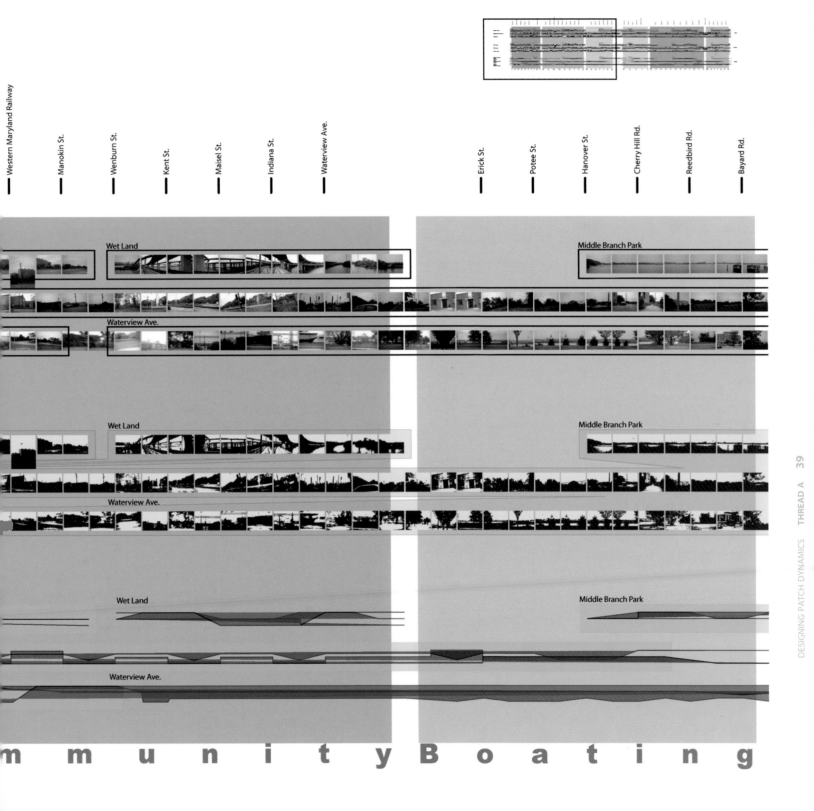

Western Maryland Railway Manokin St. Wenburn St. Kent St. Maisel St. Indiana St. Waterview Ave. Erick St. Potee St. Hanover St. Cherry Hill Rd. Reedbird Rd. Bayard Rd.

Wet Land   Middle Branch Park

Waterview Ave.

Wet Land   Middle Branch Park

Waterview Ave.

Wet Land   Middle Branch Park

Waterview Ave.

m m u n i t y B o a t i n g

Red oak
black gum
Red maple
Sweet gum
green ash
Black cherry

proposal

canopy layer

amelanchier

winterberry
red twigged dogwood

understory layer

«exploded forest»

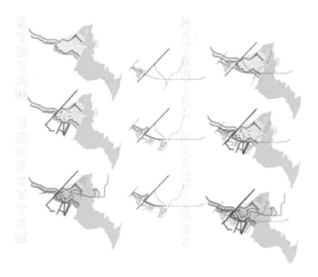

STREAM ECOSYSTEM

MATERIAL PRACTICES

Neighborhood Identities
Kratma Saini, 2002

Understanding that the perception of identity between adjacent neighborhoods is something that is not fixed but is based on individual point of view, this project proposes a new system of legibility based on something that is fixed; a greenway and watershed logic. It is a goal that, by building a new pattern of boundaries that overlaps but does not alter the existing boundaries, space is made for another layer of relationships to emerge, this time in dialogue with the natural processes that act in a neighborhood.

Taking street trees as infrastructure, I have proposed an extensive planting program that arrays fields of species in patches and corridors. Patches connect existing parks and forest areas. As the street grid often shifts and the local topography is disorienting, repetition of a limited palette of tree species acts as a medium to navigate through a neighborhood. Patches also function as a green way for plants, birds and other animals to move among ecosystems along yards and streets.

Corridors are the narrow paths that align with the watershed ridgelines and drainage lines. At the end of the corridors that meet the Gwynns Falls boundary, I have proposed water settling ponds that have multiple overlapping programs. These include: sediment settlement, day lighting the hidden path of neighborhood water, a marker of a trail head to Gwynns Falls Trail, storage for a street tree water program and a slow water recreation park.

Neighborhood Conectivities
Pavitrhra Sriprakash, 2002

Located at the mouth of Gwynns Falls where it discharges into the Middle Branch, this project is already sited in a place of meeting. The scheme is comprised of terraces of boundary elements that make connections between the urban stream and the stream ecosystem. In particular it is the slow deposition of these two streams that allows for new relationships of meeting to emerge, this time between people and the two types of water.

Hidden by the spaghetti of infrastructure that crosses it and the industrial landscapes that abut it, this project has two sites for spatial and temporal connection that I wanted to engage. To address the upper level, I have proposed a process of cutting away the canalization of the river to allow for the process of flooding to register and therefore be seen from the highway. This allows for a place of two times, a new boundary between the slow speed of the highway peak hour and the flow of rainwater.

The lower level is a place of embodied flow. Abandoned railway lines and overgrown roads are opened as public pathways in concert with the project of spreading of the flow water over shallow terraces. This first phase is a movement of long slow overlap and exploration. With the next two phases of extension, the street grid, mixed use housing and public garden terraces transform the overlap landscape into shifting boundaries of activity. These new boundaries adjust in relationship to flood levels as movement across the water can be closed or muddy, and movement away from water is onto vertical picnic towers.

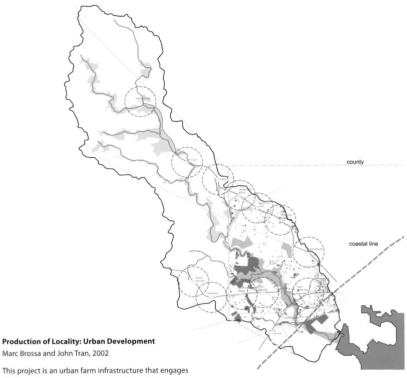

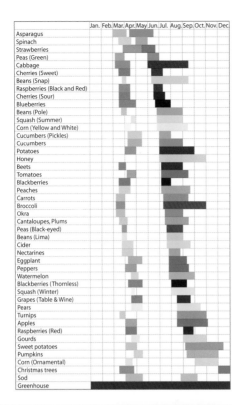

Production of Locality: Urban Development
Marc Brossa and John Tran, 2002

This project is an urban farm infrastructure that engages the flow of water as a public amenity. It is an infill planted landscape, in which flowering, fruiting, and in particular moments of harvest foster shifting perceptions of local scale. Understood as a spatio-temporal landscape, the neighborhood is navigated by rhythms of flooding and draining, harvest and decay, commuting and play.

Rather than creating boundaries, this project is made visible in the watershed by increasingly dense clusters of overlapping layers of infrastructure. Taking the latent potential of the proposed storm-sewer separation project by the city of Baltimore, the process of street excavation is understood as the first step toward harvesting of urban surface water.

By keeping an engineering logic of draining, water is temporarily stored in the street. Each farm, created by strategic consolidation of vacant lots and abandoned buildings, drains this water. The topography of the watershed is registered in deep and narrow street scale pools of storage and flow. Two additional patterns of connection to the water-harvesting network are sprinklers and hoses for local gardens and street trees.
The mechanism for this vision came from a detailed material study for the Franklin Square neighborhood. The densest zone of land cultivation and exposed water harvesting infrastructure is within a ten-minute walking distance of the local train station. Harvested produce is sold locally as well as being transported to the markets.

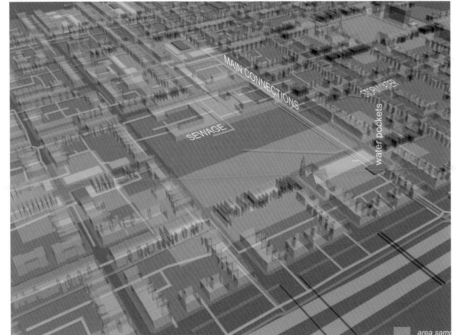

CHAPTER II

APROPOS "PATCH DYNAMICS": NOTES ON INDETERMINACY AS OPERATIONAL PHILOSOPHY IN DESIGN

RICHARD PLUNZ

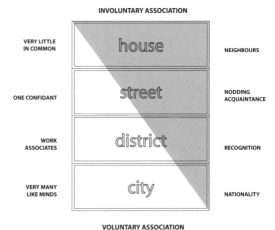

INVOLUNTARY ASSOCIATION

VERY LITTLE IN COMMON — house — NEIGHBOURS

ONE CONFIDANT — street — NODDING ACQUAINTANCE

WORK ASSOCIATES — district — RECOGNITION

VERY MANY LIKE MINDS — city — NATIONALITY

VOLUNTARY ASSOCIATION

Figure 14. "Association." Interaction between scales of human activity correlated with scales of built environment (Redrawn from Smithson, Alison and Peter 1957)

Figure 15. "Stem." Informal association in response to human activity within a flexible hexagonal infrastructure (Redrawn from Woods, Shadrach 1959)

An important aspect of the past half-century of innovation in design techniques at the urban scale has in one way or another focused on issues of formal indeterminacy, especially given the increasingly complex considerations involving prediction. For example, tools for large-scale physical design inherited from industrial era urbanization proved inadequate to respond to the complexities of new urban economies. Old strategies of in-filling static master plans obsolesced everywhere, as put in evidence by the frequency of their adjustment or complete annulment whenever investment opportunities dictate otherwise. In fact, cities within the most advanced economies now are obliged to maintain parallel strategic plans such that the master plan overrides can be more easily accommodated given the realities of fiscal liquidity and physical indeterminacy. Theoretical perspectives have moved in tandem, such that in recent decades the problem of formal determinacy has engaged several philosophical sensibilities relative to urban operations in space-time. To facilitate this review, these sensibilities are categorized into three tendencies: the "Proto-Organic," the "Geo-Political," and the "Mathematical/Informational." Each engages philosophy more than precise method. They have been crucial to the continuing discourse on new urban design techniques and especially with the advent of new digital tools, they increasingly move toward the operational as well as the conceptual. One can say the same for the concept of the patch dynamic which has emerged from the field of ecological studies and is integral to the Baltimore Ecosystem Study.

The Proto-Organic emerges from the desire to find a predictive tool which can mirror certain "naturalistic" tendencies in urban growth - usually managed through physical infrastructural configuration which allows an evolution of fabric in conformity with forces not always predictable in their precise formal outcomes. The Geo-Political concentrates on social infrastructure as a primary predictive element in urban form-making. That range of considerations is broadly based, from social organization as direct model for physical form to precedent-based historical/cultural models. The Mathematical/

Informational deploys feedback simulation of environmental change such that outcomes are predicted and altered depending on the value system at hand. This last tendency is more recent than the first two, dependent as it is on developments in information technology and related to the evolution of the field of cybernetics. Of course, to some degree all three sensibilities are interrelated; one can find something of each in almost any larger-scale strategic urban design thinking. What follows are several exemplars for each, in the order of their chronological development leading up to the late 1970s when the concept of "patch dynamics" first emerged within ecological studies and, in a sense, began to complement the discourse in architecture and urban design.

Proto-Organic

The Proto-Organic tendency emerged from the structural inadequacies of the Cartesian formalism which had been widely deployed in the gridiron planning of the 19th century city. Its application stretches back to include such approaches as Camillo Sitte's landmark *City Building According to Artistic Principles* (1889). By the mid-20th century, the new movement infrastructures associated with the automobile presented a renewed urgency for revised strategies. The studies of Peter and Alison Smithson, including the London Roads Net ("Cluster City" 1957), pioneered urban geometric organization in order to accommodate the new movement imperatives. The Smithsons recognized other new infrastructural requirements as well, notably related to new scales of societal organization (Figure 14). In France, Shadrach Woods investigated into continuous urban form as an alternative to the point-block high-rise which had come to dominate the post-World War II large scale urban project ("Stem and Web" 1959, Figure 15). Inherent to these explorations of new geometries was the desire for infrastructural flexibility in response to socialization and movement hierarchies. Elsewhere the redeployment of precedents related to "indigenous" growth became important, including their implications for micro-scale urban intervention. In England, Gordon Cullen explored new variations of the picturesque urban landscape

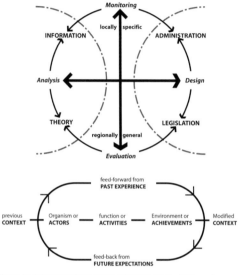

Figure 16. "Elements of Change" and "Housing Process." Schema for causal relationships between analysis and design; and monitoring and evaluation (Redrawn from Turner, John F. C. 1976)

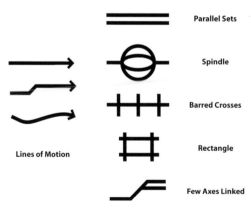

Figure 17. "Designing the Paths" and "Lines of Motion." Visual hierarchy of movement infrastructure as analog to functional hierarchies. (Redrawn from Lynch, Kevin 1960)

("Townscape" 1961), following that aspect of the Sitte-esque strategy which used the picturesque as a foil to the Cartesian grid.

Other forms of the Proto-Organic derived from the building process itself, especially in the realm of housing production. Researching the phenomenon of rapid urbanization in Latin America, John F. C. Turner concentrated on learning from the processes of so-called spontaneous growth (Figure 16) towards a better understanding of how to harness this energy and enhance its political attributes ("Self-Build" 1963). In the Netherlands, N. John Habraken sought to rationalize processes relative to advanced building economies and technologies ("Supports" 1964), such that formal and technological infrastructure could provide a framework for a quasi-indeterminate housing infill. Similar concerns, employing a far more utopian language came from Peter Cook in London ("Plug-In City" 1964). Cook envisioned city-building as the application of a kit of interchangeable modules. At a more experiential level in the United States, Kevin Lynch's work began to explore urban infrastructure related to sensory dynamics with perceptual shifting and adjusting within a space-time continuum ("Image" 1960, Figure 17). Over the next two decades, this phenomenological sensibility in urbanism became pronounced, notably in the work of Christian Norberg-Schultz in Norway ("Genius Loci" 1979).

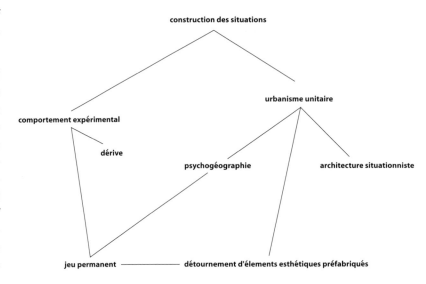

Figure 18. "Construction Des Situations." Psycho-geography becomes a central ingredient for design as critical inquiry. (Redrawn from Situationist International 1958)

Figure 19 (opposite). "Form Types" and "Four of the Five Basic Operations." Urban Metabolics based on form-types and formal operations. (Redrawn from Maki, Fumihiko 1967)

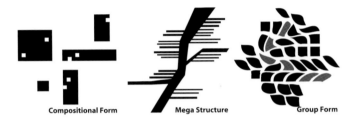

Compositional Form   **Mega Structure**   **Group Form**

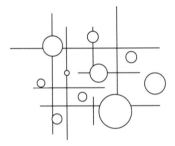

Mediate:
Connect with internate elements or intermedium (including

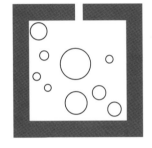

Define:
Enclose disparate structures with a sensible barrier. Produce unity within the barrier and separate from what is out side.

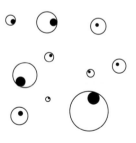

Repeat:
Give each element a feacommon to all in the ground each is identified as part of same order.

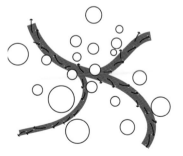

Make a Sequential Path:
Place activities that are sequence in identifiable s relation to one another.

Geo-Political

Many of the above schemes were dependent on a dimension of Geo-Political consensus, putting in evidence not only the limitations of Cartesian formalism, but also the confines of human behavioral models. Beginning in the 1940s, sociology had begun to articulate, at a theoretical level, the concept of group dynamics as a structural force in environmental change. For example, Kurt Lewin's work on "field theory" was seen as part of a new approach to the definition of a "social ecology" ("Psychological Ecology" 1943). By the 1960s, the more overt tendencies toward the Geo-Political placed additional emphasis on the definition of "community" in the evolution of the urban operation - in the broadest political sense. Within a certain utopian critical tradition in the United States, the work of Paul and Percival Goodman pioneered the strategy of deployment of political infrastructure as critical urban form-giver ("Communitas" 1947). In Europe, the Situationists, including Guy DeBord, further explored this reading of urbanism as a form of critical inquiry, especially relative to the emerging post-war consumer society (Figure 18). In France, Constant would explore this idea to its most avant-gardist conceptual limitations ("New Babylon" 1956), and in the vast post-war re-urbanizations of Japan, Kenzo Tange and others pushed the scale of urban form-making to its physical limits ("Metabolism" 1960).

The formal merging of the geopolitical and organic in the '60s was perhaps most notable in Japan. A prominent example is Fumihiko Maki's early work on invention of a lexicon of "form types" as a crucial ingredient to "basic operations" ("Collective Form" 1967, Figure 19). The evolution of the Geo-Political in the United States tended to remain more in the realm of process, as in the strategies articulated by Paul Davidoff ("Advocacy" 1965). From Europe came a stronger notion of urban form as a social contract. Especially in the theories of Italian Aldo Rossi in Italy ("Città Analoga" 1966), the importance of historical continuity was paramount in the sense that historical knowledge of the urban artifact was expected to play a defining role in its future evolution. In this regard, Rome became central to the similar, if more historicist, theories of Colin Rowe ("Collage City" 1978) which strategized around the public good inherent to the re-contextualization of historic fabrics including the modern. On the other hand, Cedric Price in England foresaw the disruption of historical consensus as a form of collective "shock" therapy to stimulate the re-development of obsolescing urban fabrics ("Non-Plan" 1969).

Mathematical/Informational

The Mathematical/Informational directly engages cybernetics - the study of information

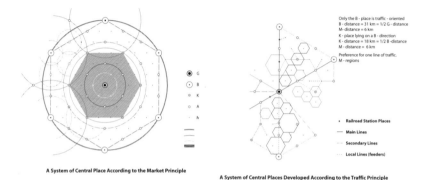

Figure 20. "Central Place Market Principle" and "Traffic Principle." Dynamic modeling of exchange of goods at the regional scale. (Redrawn from Christaller, Walter 1933)

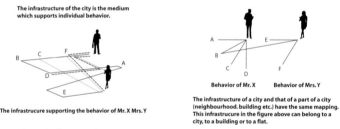

Figure 21. "Behavioral Infrastructure." Multi-scalar infrastructure as medium for individual behavior. (Redrawn from Friedman, Yona 1958)

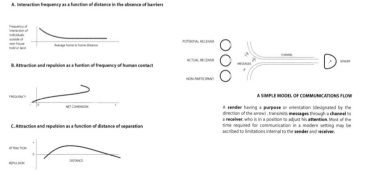

Figure 22. "Communications Flow" and "Community Growth." Urban growth and change as by-product of communications dynamics. (Redrawn from Meier, Richard L. 1962)

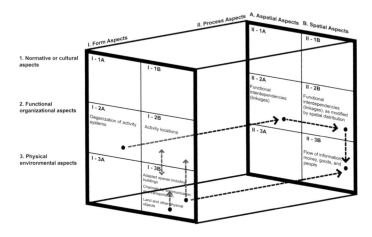

Figure 23. "Spatial Structure Trichotomy." Spatial-temporal matrix interrelating communication, function, and human association. (Redrawn from Webber, Melvin 1964)

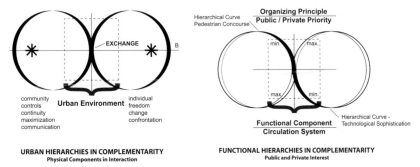

Figure 24. "Yale Model." Urban growth and change as dynamic dialectic interaction of environmental attributes. (Redrawn from Chermayeff, Serge 1965)

science which emerged out of the technological advances of the Second World War - most importantly radar and other electronic technology applications involving feedback loops. Several widely influential theoretical texts emerged from information science, including Norbert Weiner's *Cybernetics* (1948), Claude Shannon and Warren Weaver's *The Mathematical Theory of Communication* (1949), Ross Ashby's *Design for a Brain* (1952), and Anatol Rapoport's *Operational Philosophy* (1953). These speculations complemented certain pioneering works in linguistics such as Noam Chomsky's *Aspects of the Theory of Syntax* (1965). New directions emerged related to the fields of geology and ecology, making obvious the potential for application of information science to the design of the physical environment. In this regard, of early importance was the work of Walter Christaller in Germany on dynamic modeling of regional functional concentrations ("Central Place" 1933). His model demonstrated the conceptual efficacy of controlling indeterminacy at the regional scale through a flexible informational infrastructure such that the change of state in any component of the system could predict resultant change elsewhere in the system (Figure 20). Toward the end of the 1950s, diverse models proliferated within these general conceptual parameters. In France, Yona Friedman explored the idea of an informational infrastructure for the urban scale (Figure 21) in which the urban fabric could respond to changing patterns of desire ("Mobile City" 1958). In the United States, Richard L. Meier put forth the notion of a generalized communication theory for urban growth ("Communication" 1962, Figure 22), and Melvin Webber advanced the proposition of an emerging non-centroidal interpretation of urban infrastructure which could be activated by management of activity ("NonPlace" 1964, Figure 23).

The pioneering design studies of Serge Chermayeff further elaborated an operational basis for the Mathematical/Informational sensibility through the development of a dialectic approach to infrastructure seeking a state of equilibrium between bi-polar "opposite" environmental characteristics, layered into shifting urban mosaics ("Urban Complimentarity" 1965, Figure 24). The first iteration of this dialectic modeling emerged with the publication of Chermayeff and Christopher Alexander's *Community and Privacy* (1963), which is significant in that it was digitized - the first such application of the computer as a design tool for architecture and urban design. Chermayeff and Alexander anticipated the correlation of a broad range of functional criteria to produce a lexicon of patterns whose relative dominance depended on the particular problem sets under consideration (Figure 25). Thus began the notion of predictive design using digital tools to test various formal outcome scenarios. The

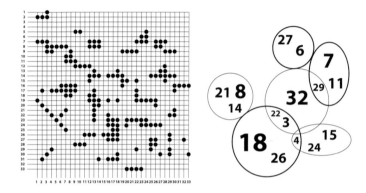

Figure 25. "Interaction and Constellation of Functional Requirements." Spatial pattern-making through correlation of functional requirements. (Redrawn from Chermayeff, Serge, and Christopher Alexander 1963)

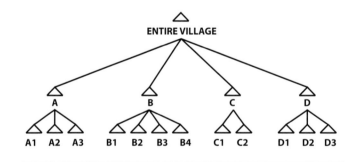

A1 contains requirements 7, 53, 57, 59, 60, 72, 125, 126, 128.
A2 contains requirements 31, 34, 36, 52, 54, 80, 94, 106, 136.
A3 contains requirements 37, 38, 50, 55, 77, 91, 103.
B1 contains requirements 39, 40, 41, 44, 51, 118, 127, 131, 138.
B2 contains requirements 30, 35, 46, 47, 61, 97, 98.

Figure 26. "Village Tree." Environmental structure as composite hierarchy of functional requirements.(Redrawn from Alexander, Christopher 1967)

URBAN 5

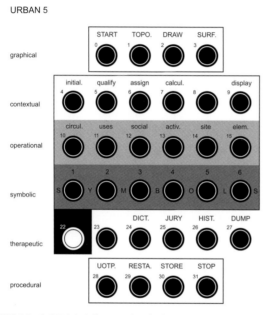

Figure 27. "URBAN 5 Overlay." Digital window as medium for dynamic interaction of environmental characteristics. (Redrawn from Negroponte, Nicholas 1968)

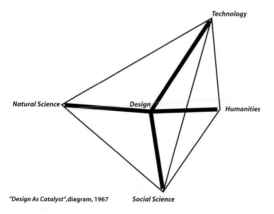

Figure 28. "Design as Catalyst." Design prototyping as catalyst for environmental problem-solving across disciplines. (Redrawn from Chermayeff, Serge 1974)

work prefigured the concentration on "design methods" of the following decade or so, not the least of which was Alexander's continuing exploration of the formal language needed to mediate between digital description and the design configuration ("Pattern Language" 1967, Figure 26). At a more speculative level in France, Nicholas Schöffer envisioned entire cities formulated as a kind of informational mainframe transforming themselves with a degree of formal fluidity never before possible ("Ville Cybernetique" 1969). And in the United States, Nicholas Negroponte engaged similar speculation at the architectural scale, with more emphasis on formal negotiation via software construction ("URBAN 5" 1968, Figure 27).

Within the shifting worlds of design fashion in the 1970s, the above-mentioned realm of conceptual research was not sustained. Other newly emerging environmental disciplines, however, began to explore similar sensibilities. From landscape architecture came Ian McHarg's *Design with Nature* (1969) which, apart from expanding the discourse on design coming from "designers," further pioneered the technique of layering as analytic strategy. Notable within the context of this chapter was the increasingly articulated realm of ecological studies evolving as a form of social science, especially for the urban realm. Specifically, the concept of the "shifting mosaic" of pattern language reappeared in the work of Steward T.A. Pickett, John N. Thompson, and others ("Patch Dynamics" 1978). A parallel discourse evolved around urban ecology and the challenge of modeling the dynamics of natural systems focused on the indeterminacies of disturbance. At least at the level of philosophical tendencies, the urban design and ecological disciplines began to share the domains of pattern languages, patch equilibriums, and shifting mosaics. And by the 1990s, some of the sensibility of Kurt Lewin's "psychological ecology" evolved within the emerging fields of urban ecology. The catalyst of urbanism further developed certain affinities between designers and naturalists, leading to the concept of "landscape urbanism." Understanding this new urban ecology entailed the vicissitudes of human intervention such that the complexities of "disturbance" changed the discourse, and, as with the field of urban design, the conceptual modeling of the urban ecosystem faced the question of intervention as an integral piece of the equation - hence the importance of "design" as catalyst and the discovery of shared domain between the disciplines (Figure 28). An informal maxim emerged that to intervene one must design, to design one must predict, and to predict one must simulate.

At this point in the evolution of intervention for both the so-called "natural" and "urban" landscapes, the least developed domain belongs to simulation. Over the past forty years the design activity which has remained the province of traditional designers has resisted integration such that simulation software has failed to move beyond simple forms of spatial representation. The precise correlation of social-functional factors with design outcomes has not been obtained in spite of the theoretical groundwork of the '60s and the digital breakthroughs of the '90s. Within the province of the design disciplines, the digital revolution has been more in the realm of Hollywood than of the social sciences. In this regard, the ecological component has been useful in breaking the bubble of traditional design determinants. This notion of design in an expanded field carries with it a catalytic function relative to other fields - especially true for the urban sphere, where a crucial part of any operation entails a social contract, in which political consensus is an inevitable prerequisite for any intervention. Political consensus inevitably requires illustrative formal outcomes, such that the imperative for design is the catalyst among many stakeholders.

Note: The basis for this chapter originated with a Columbia University seminar, #A4697: Philosophies of Urban Operations, taught by the author in the spring semester of 1999.

References

Proto-Organic:

Cluster City. 1957. Alison and Peter Smithson.

Smithson, Alison and Peter. 1967. Urban Structuring. London: Studio Vista.

Smithson, Alison and Peter. 1973. Without Rhetoric An Architectural Aesthetic 1955-1972. London: Lattimer New Dimensions, Ltd. p 91-117, 140-159.

Smithson, Alison, editor. 1991. Team 10 Meetings, 1953-1984. New York: Rizzoli.

Stem and Web. 1959. Shadrach Woods.

Newman, Oscar, editor. 1961. CIAM '59 in Otterloo. Stuttgart: Karl Krämer Verlag.

Woods, Shadrach, editor. 1968. Candilis-Josic-Woods: Building for People. New York: Frederick A. Praeger.

CIAM 10 Issue. May 1960. Architectural Design 30.

Townscape. 1961. Gordon Cullen.

Cullen, Gordon. 1961. Townscape. London: The Architectural Press. pp. 9-15.

Self-Build. 1963. John F.C. Turner.

Turner, John F.C. August 1963. Dwelling Resources in South America. Architectural Design 33.

Turner, John F.C. 1976. Housing by People: Towards Autonomy in Building Environments. London: Marion Boyars,. pp. 3-34, 160-169.

Supports. 1964. N. John Habraken.

Habraken, N. John. 1972. SUPPORTS: An Alternative to Mass Housing. New York: Praeger Publishers. pp. 4-39.

Habraken, N.J., et al. 1976. VARIATIONS: The Systemmatic Design of Supports. Cambridge, Mass: MIT Laboratory of Architecture and Planning.

Plug-in City. 1964. Peter Cook et.al.

Cook, Peter. 1970. Experimental Architecture. New York: Universe Books. pp. 96-111; 112-132.

Cook, Peter. 1967. Architecture: Action and Plan. London: Studio Vista.

Image. 1960. Kevin Lynch.

Lynch, Kevin. 1960. The Image of the City. Cambridge, Mass: The MIT Press.

Lynch, Kevin. 1981. A Theory of Good Urban Form. Cambridge, Mass: The MIT Press.

Genius Loci. 1979. Christian Norberg-Schulz.

Norberg-Schulz, Christian.1966. Intentions in Architecture. Oslo: Universitetsforlaqet.

Norberg-Schulz, Christian. 1980. Genius Loci: Towards a Phenomenology of Architecture. New York: Rizzoli. pp. 50-78.

Geo-Political:

Communitas. 1947. Paul and Percival Goodman.

Goodman, Paul and Percival. 1947. Communitas: Means of Livelihood and Ways of Life. Chicago: University of Chicago Press. pp. 1-15.

New Babylon. 1956. Constant.

Constant. 1996. New Babylon. In Andreotti, Libero and Xavier Costa, editors. Theory of the Dérive and Other Situationist Writings on the City. Barcelona: ACTAR. pp. 154-169.

Metabolism. 1960. Kenzo Tange, et al.

Maki, Fumihiko. 1967. Investigations in Collective Form. St. Louis: Washington University School of Architecture. pp. 3-51.

Metabolist Issue. October 1964. Architectural Design 34.

Advocacy. 1965. Paul Davidoff.

Cloward, Richard A. and Richard M. Elman. 1967. The Storefront on Stanton Street: Advocacy in the Ghetto, In Brager, George A. and Francis D. Purcell, editors. Community Action Against Poverty. New Haven: College and University Press.

Davidoff, Paul. November 1965. Advocacy and Pluralism in Planning. American Institute of Planners Journal: 31. pp. 331-338.

Davidoff, Paul. 1967. Democratic Planning, Perspecta 11. pp. 156-159.

Fox Piven, Frances. 1971. Regulating the Poor. New York: Pantheon Books.

Goodman, Robert. 1972. After the Planners. New York: Simon and Schuster.

Città Analoga. 1966. Aldo Rossi.

Rossi, Aldo. 1982. The Architecture of the City. Cambridge, Mass: The MIT Press. pp. 29-61.

Rossi, Aldo. 1976. La Città Analoga: Tavola, Lotus International: 13. pp. 4-9.

Non-Plan. 1969. Cedric Price.

Price, Cedric. October1966. Potteries Thinkbelt. Architectural Design: 36. pp. 484-497.

Price, Cedric. May 1969. Non-Plan. Architectural Design: 39. pp. 269-273.

Collage City. 1978. Colin Rowe.

Graves, Michael, editor. 1979. Roma Interotta. AD Profiles: 20.

Rowe, Colin and Fred Koetter. 1978. Collage City. Cambridge, Mass: The MIT Press. pp. 86-117.

Mathematical/Informational:

Central Place. 1933. Walter Christaller.

Christaller, Walter. 1966. Central Places in Southern Germany. Englewood Cliffs: Prentice-Hall, Inc. pp. 27-83.

Foley, Donald L. 1964. An Approach to Metropolitan Spatial Structure. In Webber, Melvin, editor. Explorations Into Urban Structure. Philadelphia: University of Pennsylvania Press. pp. 21-78.

Mobile City. 1958. Yona Friedman.

Friedman, Yona. 1970. L'Architecture Mobile: Vers une Cité Concue par ses Habitants. Tournai: Casterman.

Friedman, Yona. 1975. Toward A Scientific Architecture. Cambridge, Mass: The MIT Press. pp. 62-92; 110-123.

Communication. 1962. Richard L. Meier.

Meier, Richard L. 1965. Developmental Planning. New York: McGraw-Hill.

Meier, Richard L. 1962. A Communications Theory of Urban Growth. Cambridge, Mass: The Joint Center for Urban Studies. pp. 1-44.

Nonplace. 1964. Melvin Webber.

Webber, Melvin. 1964. Urban Place and the Nonplace Urban Realm. In Webber, Melvin, editor. Explorations Into Urban Structure. Philadelphia: University of Pennsylvania Press. pp. 79-153.

Urban Complementarity. 1965. Serge Chermayeff.

Chermayeff, Serge and Christopher Alexander. 1963. Community and Privacy: Toward a New Architecture of Humanism. Garden City: Doubleday and Company, Inc.

Chermayeff, Serge and Alexander Tzonis. 1967. Advanced Studies in Urban Environments: Toward An Urban Model. New Haven: Yale University. pp. 143-153.

Chermayeff, Serge and Alexander Tzonis. 1971. Shape of Community: Realization of Human Potential. Baltimore: Penguin Books Inc.

Mitchell, W. editor. January 1969. Synopsis of Conclusions and Record of Process: The Chermayeff Studio. Autumn 1968-69. New Haven: Yale University School of Arts and Architecture.

Pattern Language. 1967. Christopher Alexander.

Alexander, Christopher. 1977. A Pattern Language: Towns, Buildings, Construction. New York: Oxford University Press.

Alexander, Christopher. 1968. A Pattern Language Which Generates Multi-Service Centers. Berkeley: Center for Environmental Structure.

Alexander, Christopher. 1967. Notes on the Synthesis of Form. Cambridge, Mass: Harvard University Press. pp. 73-94.

Alexander, Christopher, Sara Ishikawa, and Murray Silverstein. 1969. Houses Generated by Patterns. Berkeley: Center for Environmental Structure.

Ville Cybernetique. 1969. Nicolas Schöffer.

Schöffer, Nicolas. 1963. Space, Light, Time. Neuchatel: Editions du Griffon.

Schöffer, Nicolas.1969. La Ville Cybernetique. Paris: Tchou. pp. 99-136.

Architecture Machine. 1970. Nicholas Negroponte.

Negroponte, Nicholas. 1970. The Architecture Machine: Toward a More Humane Environment. Cambridge, Mass: The MIT Press. pp. 71-93; 95-117.

Negroponte, Nicholas. 1995. Being Digital. New York: Knopf.

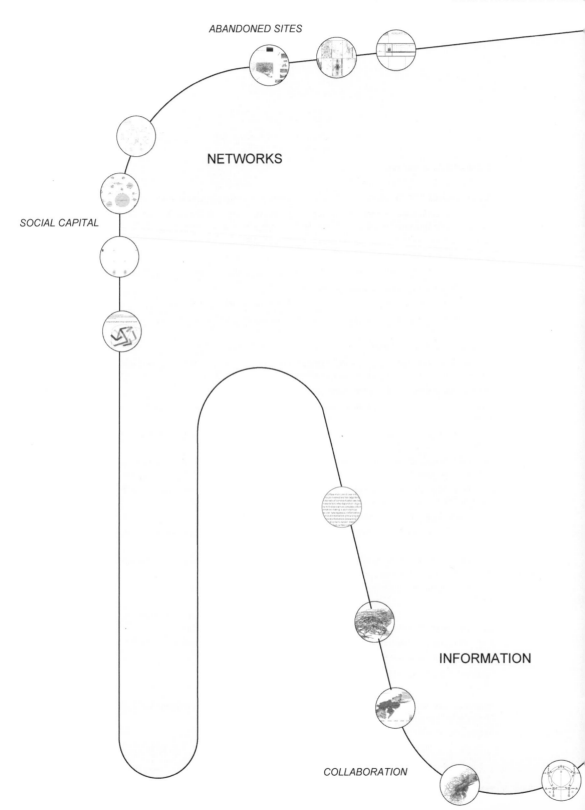

SOCIAL-NATURAL INDICATO

ABANDONED SITES

NETWORKS

SOCIAL CAPITAL

INFORMATION

COLLABORATION

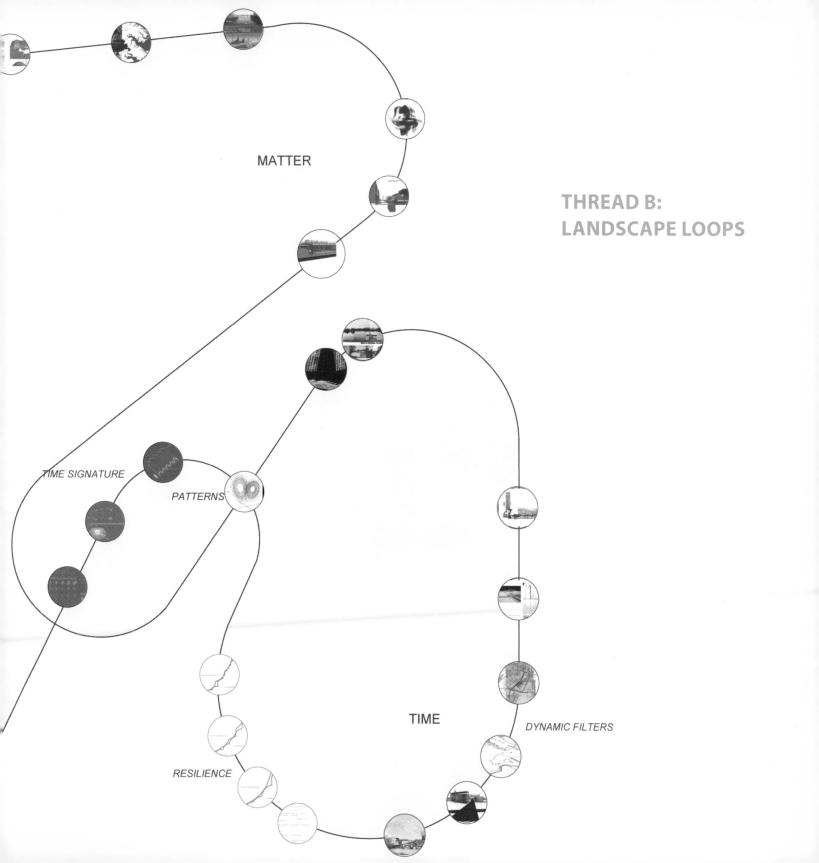

MATTER

THREAD B:
LANDSCAPE LOOPS

TIME SIGNATURE

PATTERNS

RESILIENCE

TIME

DYNAMIC FILTERS

ARCHITECTURE STUDIO WORK 2002, GWYNNS FALLS WATERSHED.
Richard Plunz, Critic. Brian Abell, Tomasz Adach, Katherine Chang, Sari Kronish, Raphael Levy, Carolyn Walls, Students.

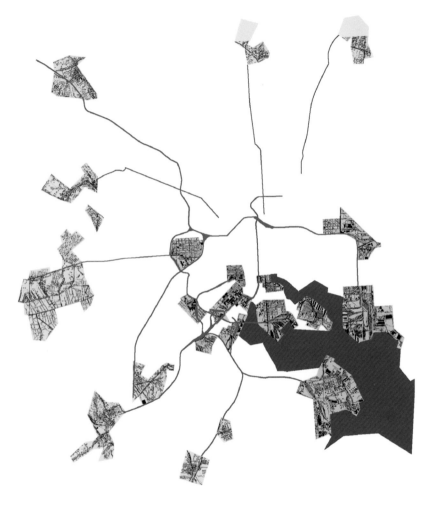

Peripheral Landscape: Regional growth induced by infra-structure, circa 1900
Brian Abell, 2002

Peripheral Landscape (opposite)
Brian Abell, 2002

Urban Patch Dynamics: Gwynns Falls Assemblage
Excerpts from the Studio Briefs and Projects

On the Studio in General: Our research envisions an urbanism comprising operationally connected sets of patches with temporarily and spatially viable attributes. Building on this approach, our work will explore man-made ecologies in Baltimore related to urban form and socio-economic domains, with particular emphasis on parameters emanating from those architectural design parameters that are related to urban form.

The work of the studio is subdivided chronologically into two areas of investigation: 1) design of an overall contextual concept for the Gwynns Falls watershed corridor with application of the patch dynamic concept; 2) design of an "architectonic fragment" for the Middle Branch Park in the form of a social condenser which illustrates the catalytic effects of a patch interaction. We emphasize revaluing the city through landscape; and integrative investigation between designers and ecologists incorporating "physical, biotic and social attributes" of the city.

On the Theoretical Premise: Prevailing theories of "patch dynamics" have originated within the natural sciences relative to the ecological consequences of environmental change. Recognition of the importance of the urban landscape relative to further development of conceptual models for understanding ecological change has led to the need to explore the concept of "patch theory" inclusive of urban social economic factors and built environment spatial dynamics. This studio explores these possibilities in conjunction with an on-going urban ecological research and planning project in Baltimore undertaken by the Institute of Ecosystem Studies with the Northeastern Research Station of the U. S. Department of Agriculture Forest Service. This research envisions a "landscape urbanism" comprising operationally connected sets of patches with "temporarily and spatially viable attributes." These sets "may be destroyed and reformed by disturbance processes, and the state of any patch is at least partially dependent on surrounding and distant patches," with "distinct assemblages of vegetation, urban form, and socioeconomic characteristics" as an "urban catena." (from Pickett, et. al.) Within the context of our work, the definition of "patch" will be viewed as an urban micro-territory within a physical morphology.

On the Baltimore Context: The site for this studio investigation is the area of influence of the Gwynns Falls watershed corridor in Baltimore, reflecting the focus of study to date by the Parks and People Foundation. This watershed represents an assemblage of archetypal urban conditions entailing a Valley Section dialectic (after Patrick Geddes) inclusive of urban and sub-urban, wealth and poverty, historic and post-historic, etc. Study to date has emphasized natural and social ecologies, to which we will add a discourse on built-form ecologies. It is important to understand the Baltimore context as an entropic zone, having once been a major North American port and industrial power; and now reduced in population from 1.2 million in the 1950's to half that number today. Baltimore shares characteristics with other older cities of industrial origin, but with perhaps a greater stratification than many along income and ethnic lines. In recent decades Baltimore has pursued a number of precedent-setting development initiatives related to the historic city center, and it remains an important node within the northeast megalopolis corridor.

On Program Specifics: The "architectonic fragment" which culminates this studio production will be a "social condenser" to be located on one of several brownfield sites along the Gwynns Falls corridor. The architectural conception of "social condenser" is meant to build on the long historical discourse on this subject: from Fourier's Phalanx (1799); to Melnikov's Workers' Clubs (1925); to Paul and Percival Goodman's Communitas (1947). Each designer will interrogate the possibilities of social condenser in the 21st century, sited on a brown field remnant of the 20th century and informed by a programmatic concept related to an interactive "patch dynamic" context for the corridor. Each designer must arrange the pieces of the puzzle according to their own system derived from the various theoretical concepts introduced to the studio whole.

Remediation Condenser: Middle Branch social/ physical remediation in six stages (opposite)
Kathy Chang, 2002

Remediation Condenser: Gwynns Falls Assemblage as transect
Kathy Chang, 2002

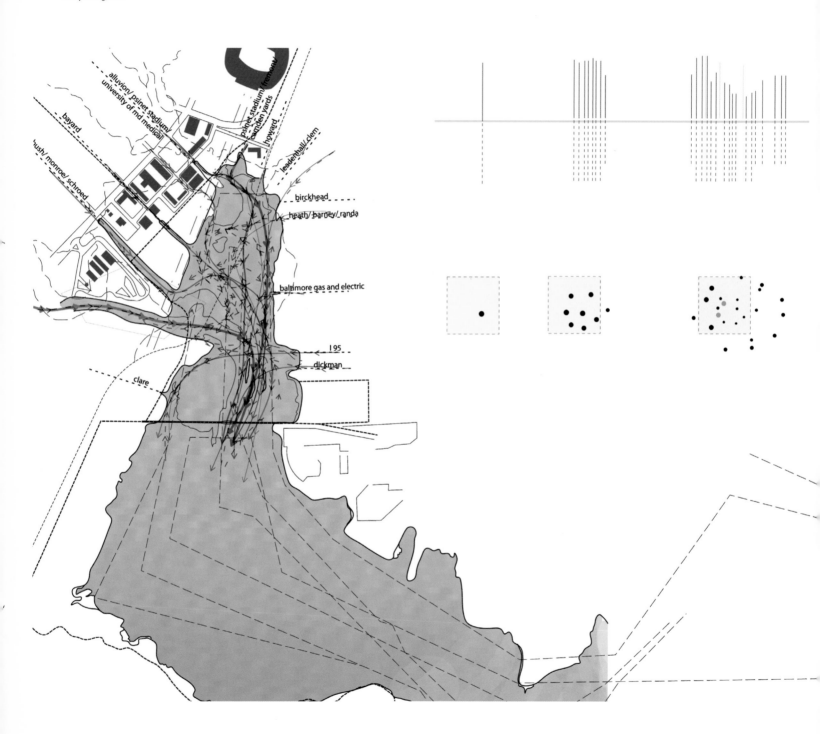

Remediation Condenser: Trash eddies with remediation nodes
Kathy Chang, 2002

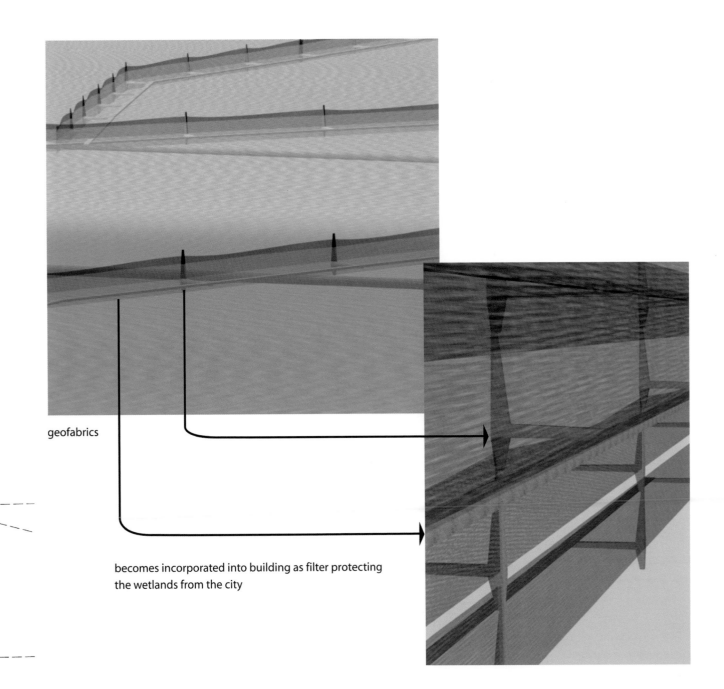

geofabrics

becomes incorporated into building as filter protecting
the wetlands from the city

Connective Landscape: Parking as an antidote to Inner Harbor, with eco-industrial park and green park (this page and opposite page)
Raphael Levy, 2002

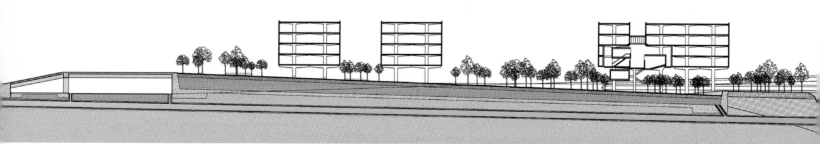

DESIGNING PATCH DYNAMICS   **THREAD B**   **63**

**Multi-Nodal Flows: Middle Branch as
resonant catch basin**
Sari Kronish, 2002

**Multi-Nodal Flows: Interconnective
grain at the regional scale**
Sari Kronish, 2002

● Water Sampling Stations
■ Existing Social Facilities
1. Botanical Garden
2. Botanical Garden + Conservatory
3. Family Fun Center
4. Skateboard Park
5. Rowing Club
6. Senior Center
7. Nature Center

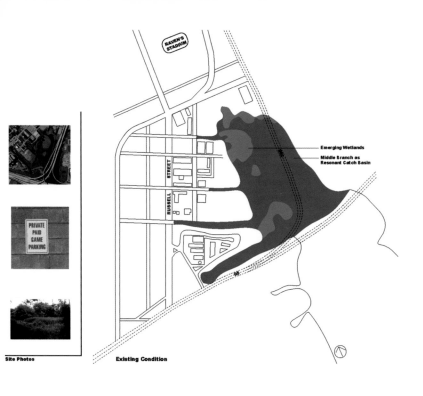

Emerging Wetlands

Middle Branch as
Resonant Catch Basin

Existing Condition

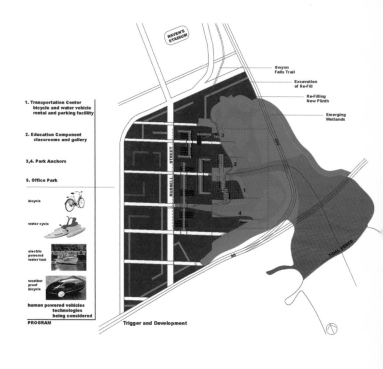

1. Transportation Center
   bicycle and water vehicle
   rental and parking facillity

2. Education Component
   classrooms and gallery

3,4. Park Anchors

5. Office Park

bicycle

water cycle

electric
powered
water taxi

weather
proof
bicycle

human powered vehicles
technologies
being considered

PROGRAM

Gwynn
Falls Trail

Excavation
of Re-Fill

Re-Filling
New Plinth

Emerging
Wetlands

Trigger and Development

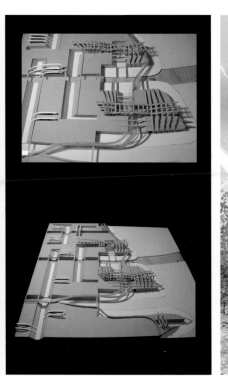

**Multi-Nodal Flows: Middle Branch
reclamation phasing (top left)**
Sari Kronish, 2002

**Multi-Nodal Flows: Middle Branch
granular matrix**
Sari Kronish, 2002

**Vernacular Re-Metamorphosis: Education
condenser (left)**
Tomasz Adach, 2002

THE MUTUAL DEPENDENCE OF SOCIAL MEANINGS, SOCIAL CAPITAL, AND THE DESIGN OF URBAN GREEN INFRASTRUCTURE

J. MORGAN GROVE, WILLIAM R. BURCH, JR.,
MATTHEW WILSON, AND AMANDA W. VEMURI

Urbanization is a dominant demographic trend and an important component of global land transformation. According to a 2001 prediction, slightly more than half the world's population was predicted to reside in cities in 2005, and this figure is projected to rise to over 60% by 2025. The developed nations have more urbanized populations; close to 80% of the US population, for example, is urban. Urbanization has also resulted in a dramatic rise in the size of cities: over 300 cities have more than 1 million inhabitants and 14 megacities exceed 10 million residents (Gottdiener and Hutchinson 2001).

In addition to its global dimensions, urbanization has important implications for regional landscapes. In industrialized nations the conversion of land from wild and agricultural uses to urban and suburban settlement is growing at a faster rate than the population growth in urban areas. Cities are no longer compact; rather, they sprawl in fractal or spider-like configurations (Makse and others 1995). Consequently, urban areas increasingly abut and interdigitate with wild lands. Even for many rapidly growing metropolitan areas, suburban zones are growing faster than other zones (Katz and Bradley 1999). The resulting new forms of urban development include edge cities (Garreau 1991) and housing interspersed in forest, shrubland, and desert habitats. An essential component to this landscape transformation is the planning, design, construction, and maintenance of the built environment (Hough 1984; Spirn 1984). This built environment can be evaluated in terms of its ecological interactions. For example, how does it affect air and water quality, biodiversity, and energy use? Green infrastructure has received renewed interest over the past twenty years because of its ability to improve water quality, remediate soils, reduce energy consumption, and conserve native flora and fauna.

While the environmental benefits of green infrastructure might be important and sufficient justification, we caution that the history of urban planning and design is replete with examples of projects not built or not maintained. In other words, some types of green infrastructure are built while others are not. Some types of green infrastructure persist, while others do not.

Recognizing the potential importance of green infrastructure for conserving or restoring the ecological functions of cities, our purpose in this essay is to ask why some projects are not realized or sustained. Are there important social and ecological concepts affecting the construction and maintenance of green infrastructure that planners and designers need to consider (Burch 1988)? If so, should planners and designers adopt a "blank slate" approach in order to invest green infrastructure with social and ecological complexity? Or should they focus on an "initial conditions" approach in which they examine the existing and potential social and ecological complexity of different types of green infrastructure to determine how to plan and design it? In essence, what is socially and ecologically possible, likely, and preferable (Bell 1997)?

In this essay we introduce the concept of a community stewardship opportunity spectrum (CSOS) and explore the idea that different types of community stewardship have associated social meanings and require varied types of social capital. We provide a specific example and evidence for these linkages among a type of community stewardship (stream valley parks), social meaning, and social capital. Continuing this approach, we establish the concept of an urban park opportunity spectrum and explore the idea that different types of urban parks have their own specific associated social meanings and require different types of social capital. Subsequently, we speculate on the implementation of the Olmsted Brothers' 1904 Parks Plan for Baltimore and describe how the concepts of social meaning and social capital could be used to explain where and why segments of the 1904 Plan have and have not been built over time. We conclude by considering some of the implications of relating green infrastructure, social meanings, and social capital for the planning, design, and implementation of green infrastructure.

Green Infrastructure Part I: A Spectrum of Community Stewardship Opportunities

We propose that there is a community stewardship opportunities spectrum (CSOS) in urban areas including 1) regional forestry, 2) stream valleys, 3) large protected areas, 4) abandoned industrial areas, and 5) neighborhood areas (Grove et al. 2005).

Regional forestry land cover in the Baltimore region ranges from 2.8% in Baltimore City to 35.4% in Baltimore County, with forest land cover defined as 1) greater than 0.4 hectares, 2) 10% stocked, and 3) at least 40 meters wide. (Jenkins and Riemann 2001). Regional forestry activities focus on management for drinking water supply, stream water quality/quantity, biodiversity, recreation, wildlife habitat, and forest products (Figure 29). For instance, Baltimore has recently completed a comprehensive forest management plan for 6,880 hectares of city-owned watershed properties that addresses community issues associated with water supply, biodiversity, wildlife, recreation, and forest harvesting.

Forestry focusing on Baltimore's 140 km of *stream valleys* addresses stream water quality/quantity and recreation, particularly greenway projects in the City's three prima-

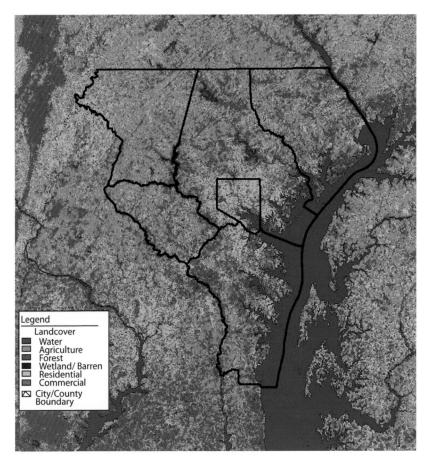

Figure 29. Land Use for the Baltimore Metropolitan Region (1990)

Figure 30. Gwynns Falls Stream Valley and Gwynns Falls & Leakin Park

Figure 31. The Gwynns Falls flows into the Middle Branch of Baltimore Harbor and the Chesapeake Bay.

Figure 32. Former Industrial Area along the Shoreline of the Middle Branch

ry watersheds: Gwynns Falls, Jones Falls, and Herring Run. Regional and stream valley forestry are frequently assessed in the context of the Chesapeake Bay watershed (Figures 30 & 31).

Forestry in *large protected areas* - parks greater than 15 hectares - deals extensively with reforestation and forest succession in order to promote aesthetics, particularly scenic qualities, water and air quality, and wildlife habitat. In these areas, forests are balanced with grass and picnic areas.

As manufacturing in Baltimore continues to decline, the number of *abandoned industrial areas* has grown. Many of these sites are along the City's harbor or adjacent to decommissioned rail lines. Numerous locations are classified as brownfields, sites identified by the U.S. Environmental Protection Agency as having low-level toxic contamination. Forestry in these areas centers on site remediation, greenway recreation along the harbor or rail-to-trail lines, and wildlife habitat (Figure 32).

Finally, forestry in *neighborhood areas* attempts to address the City's 276 neighborhoods and a range of activities including local parks, 6,500 abandoned lots, community gardens, tree nurseries, and approximately 300,000 street trees (Figures 33 & 34).

Several social concepts are associated with

Figure 33. Street trees shade residents in a Baltimore neighborhood

Figure34. An abandoned lot is converted to a Community Garden in Baltimore

each type of stewardship opportunity we propose, including social meanings, social capital, and levels of organization. We describe social meanings as a mix of beliefs, myths, identity, tastes, and values that motivate social actions. The link between social meanings and social action is important to understand; clearly, marketers build upon social meanings to encourage and entice the consumption of some things and to discourage the consumption of others (Lynes 1980; Veblen 1981 [1899]; Horowitz 1985; Glickman 1999; Halter 2000; Schor and Holt 2000; Keller and others 2002; Matt 2003).

Certain types of social capital are also associated with each type of stewardship opportunity, which we describe as the shared knowledge, understanding, norms, rules, and expectations about patterns of interactions that groups of individuals bring to a recurrent activity. Key features to the concept of social capital are that it refers to both the norms and networks that facilitate collective action. It is formed over time and embedded in common understanding rather than physical structures, and, in contrast to human capital which is embodied in individuals, social capital is embodied in social relationships. One way social meanings and social capital are linked in the context of community stewardship is by the fact that people tend to organize around things that are meaningful to them, and this is particularly true for the stewardship of the urban environment.

A final concept that we would like to introduce is the concept of scales of social organization, which Pickett and others propose to be a crucial component for understanding the biocomplexity of urban ecosystems. Scalar thinking, hierarchy theory, and panarchy theory (Holling 2001) compel us to think about how strong and weak linkages within and between scales are related to one another. Of particular interest is how lower levels of organization interact to generate higher-level behaviors and higher-level units control those at lower levels (Johnson 2001, Figure 35).

The Baltimore Ecosystem Study (BES) has worked to articulate and understand the dynamics of different social scales over time using existing social theory (Grimm and others 2000; Pickett and others 2005). Some examples of issues studied in the BES include:

1. Regional variations: urban-rural dynamics (Morrill 1974; Cronon 1991; Rusk 1993)

2. Municipal variations: distribution and dynamics of land-use change (Burgess 1925; Hoyt 1939; Harris and Ullman 1945; Guest1977)

3. Neighborhood variations: power relationships between neighborhoods (Shevky and Bell 1955 Timms 1971; Johnston 1976; Agnew 1987; Logan and Molotch 1987; Harvey 1989)

4. Household variations: household behavior within communities (Fortmann and Bruce 1988; Fox 1992, Grove and Hohmann 1992; Burch and Grove 1993; Grove 1995)

Social meanings, social capital, and social levels of organization are linked by the fact that different social meanings and types of social capital are significant at different levels of social organization (Figure36), and the social ecological resilience of urban ecosystems is likely to increase with linkages among scales (Berkes and Folke 2000; Pickett and others 2005).

Interlude I: A hypothesis of stream and watershed restoration

The development of Gwynns Falls Greenway (Figure 37) exemplifies the links between green infrastructure, social meaning, and social capital at a specific scale. It follows the following thesis of path analysis:

1. Current condition of the Gwynns Falls is a deteriorated stream with leaking infrastructure.

2. Creation of green infrastructure unique to the watershed/stream recreation resulted in a greenway trail.

3. Increased use of the greenway by locals augments their exposure to the stream and to watershed/stream "thinking," which fosters a link between neighborhood behavior, stormwater infra-

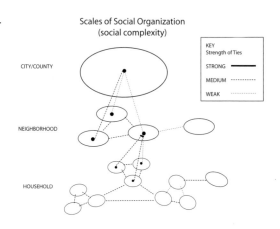

Scales of Social Organization
(social complexity)

Figure 35. Scales of Social Organization

Type of Forestry	Social Meaning	Social Capital
Regional Forestry	Drinking water, stream water, biodiversity, recreation, wildlife, forest products	Regional Planning Authorities, State Natural Resource Agencies
Stream Valleys	Stream water and recreation (Greenways)	Watershed Associations
Large, Protected Areas	Aesthetics (scenic qualities), water/air quality, wildlife, recreation (organized sports and picnics)	"Friends of X Park", Adjacent neighborood groups
Abandoned, Industrial Areas	Site remediation, recreation (Greenways), wildlife	Business Development and Recreation Groups
Neighborhood Areas	Neighborhood identity, community cohesion and stability, aesthetics, sacred spaces and memorials, produce, tree nurseries, shade	Neighborhood Groups

Figure 36. Revised Typology: Forestry, Meaning, and Capital

Figure 37. Proposed Greenway Trails for Baltimore City

structure, and stream/recreation quality.

4. The ensuing change in neighborhood behavior leads to civic support for repairing infrastructure.

5. The resulting change in stream condition is its restoration.

This thesis can be mapped to a brief history of the Gwynns Falls stream valley and its path to restoration (Groffman and others 2003).

A U.S. Army Corps of Engineers study chronicled extensive degradation of streams and riparian zones in Baltimore City, including poor riparian and in-stream habitat, stream bank and bed stability problems, and low water quality. At the same time, neighborhoods were undergoing socioeconomic decline, with the loss of nearly 50% of the population of Baltimore City between 1940 and 1990 and the abandonment of over 60,000 houses and lots. In 1994, the US Forest Service - working with local and state non-governmental organizations (NGOs); local, state, and federal agencies; and universities - established the Revitalizing Baltimore (RB) project to carry out community forestry, watershed restoration, and educational projects centered on conservation stewardship and outdoor experiences. One of the main objectives of RB was to develop the idea that ecological revitalization can stimulate socioeconomic revitalization by bringing people in underserved neighborhoods together through community forestry and stream restoration projects. These projects foster the development of community cohesion, which leads to community interest in improved city services. Increases in services engender improvements in environmental and socio-economic conditions and create positive feedback for neighborhood revitalization. This trend reverses the negative spiral of population loss with consequent environmental and social degradation which would fuel further population loss.

The idea for the Gwynns Falls trail emerged from a series of stream restoration projects and was intended to serve as a highly visible focal point for stream and neighborhood revitalization in Baltimore City. The idea was brought to fruition by the Parks and People Foundation, a non-profit group that explicitly works at the interface between humans and the environment, with a focus on creating recreational opportunities for Baltimore City residents. Parks and People coordinated fundraising activities from multiple sources in order to open the trail with great fanfare in 1999.

As more people use the trail, important feedbacks develop. Those who experience the stream and riparian zone become aware of this unique and valuable natural resource, which increases demand for its maintenance. As Baltimore Mayor Martin O'Malley noted in the *Baltimore Sun* article "A Trail Grows in Baltimore" at the opening of the second phase of the Gwynns Falls Trail, "there are all sorts of natural sights in this City that remain to be discovered by the vast majority of people" (Sun 2003). In the same article, Rose Harvey of the Trust for Public Land noted that "it really is undiscovered wilderness. I think it will allow people to connect with nature in a meaningful way." And Eric Fussel, a local resident from the adjoining neighborhood of Windsor Hills, hoped that "maybe people will begin to take pride in it [Gwynns Falls] and our neighborhood will progress rather than regress."

Our thesis linking green infrastructure, social meanings, and social capital is further supported by initial findings from our work through the Baltimore Ecosystem Study (BES). From December 4-21, 2000, we conducted a telephone survey predominantly of households living in the Gwynns Falls watershed. Questions were based upon an assortment of regional and national surveys, providing the basis for regional and national comparisons. A total of 813 surveys were completed, with the following results:

Recreation activities and watershed knowledge

More than 50% of those surveyed thought they knew in which watershed they lived. A person's watershed knowledge increased with the number of recreation activities in which s/he participated. Finally, participation in water activities influenced watershed knowledge more than participation in land based recreation activities.

Figure 38. 1904 Olmsted plan for Baltimore City

Recreation activities and willingness to participate in local environmental activities

More than 50% were likely to perform pro-environment behavior, such as support recreation fees, taxes, or legislation; volunteer to improve and maintain the quality of the local watersheds; or participate in education activities. A person's willingness to participate in local environmental behavior to improve watershed quality increased and eventually plateaued. Again, water activities were associated with increased participation more than land based recreation activities.

These survey findings provide additional empirical support for the idea that the construction and use of green infrastructure such as greenway trails can be an important tool for building awareness and support for watershed conservation and restoration, and that humans can function as a regulatory feedback mechanism in the ecosystem much as a complex web of interactions maintains stability (resistance and resilience) in unmanaged forest ecosystems (Bormann and Likens 1979; Groffman and other 2003).

Green Infrastructure Part II: A Spectrum of Urban Park Opportunities

The idea of an opportunity spectrum for urban natural resource management is not something new. Though they did not call it an opportunity spectrum, the Olmsted Brothers were articulate and compelling in their description of different types of urban parks, social meanings associated with each park type, and the appropriate plan and design of each park type for Baltimore in their 1904 Plan. For example, they identified a range of park types including 1) small parks and squares, 2) large parks, 3) stream valley parks, 4) radial parkways and cross-connections, and 5) outlying reservations. Within each of these park types, they articulated a range of purposes and social values such as a) exercise, b) playgrounds, c) grounds for little children, d) athletic fields, e) other exertive exercise, f) incidental exercise, g) social recreation, h) promenades, i) neighborly recreation, j) enjoyment of outdoor beauty, k) enjoyment of formal design, l) enjoyment of nature and m) enjoymentof natural scenery, and n) parkways (Olmsted 1987 [1904], Figure 38).

Interlude II: A hypothesis relating social capital and the construction of urban parks

The link between Parts I and II of this chapter is the fact that the Gwynns Falls Trail was part of the Olmsted's 1904 Plan, but was not implemented until 1996. The obvious question is "what caused this delay?" We think the answer to this question is inherent in the questions we first posed at the beginning of this chapter: Why are some types of green infrastructure built while others are not? Why do some types of green infrastructure persist, while others do not?

We believe that the preliminary answer to the greenway question is that while the Olmsteds developed a wonderful plan and park designs, and carefully and accurately identified the relevant social meanings, the necessary social capital did not exist until the 1990s for their plan and design to be realized. In other words, their green infrastructure proposal did not meet the requisite social conditions—plan/design, social meaning, and social capital—to be brought to fruition.

To enhance our understanding of the links among plan/design, social meaning, and social capital in green infrastructure, we propose to take the Olmsteds' 1904 plan as their social ecological hypothesis and prediction of what should exist now. In this case, if the 1904 plan and the 2004 current conditions matched perfectly, than the Olmsteds would have an R-squared value of 1.00. However, if the plan and current conditions do not match (Figure 39), we propose that parks that were proposed but either a) were not built or b) if built, were not maintained, be considered residuals (errors) of commission, and parks that were built but not planned be

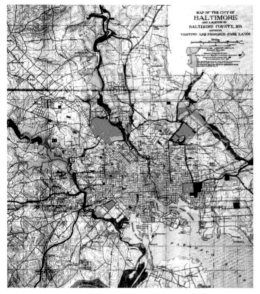

Figure 39. Overlay of Baltimore City Parks in 2004 with the Olmsted Plan in 1904

considered residuals of omission. Also, given our interest in the long-term social ecological dynamics of Baltimore, we would be interested to know both when parks were commissioned and their maintenance history—periods of maintenance and periods of no or little maintenance. The next step would be to determine whether residuals of commission are associated with the absence of social meaning or social capital, and whether the residuals of omission are associated with the presence of social meanings or social capital. We believe this research would provide a long-term understanding of the relationship between green infrastructure, social meaning, and social capital in general and Baltimore in particular.

Conclusions

In this essay we presented the idea that different types of green infrastructure have associated social meanings and social capital and that the successful plans, designs, and sustainability of green infrastructure requires an explicit understanding and analysis of relevant social meanings and social capital. In particular, our thesis is that "if you build it, they might not come." That is to say that, in some cases, the requisite social meanings and social capital do not exist and will need to be socially constructed in order to motivate action. If this thesis seems reasonable and practical, planners and designers might consider a set of follow-up questions:

• Given a desired green infrastructure, what are the necessary social meanings and social capital?

• Given existing social meanings and social capital, what are the needed green infrastructure(s)?

• Can green infrastructure respond to and create social meanings and social capital?

• What are the green infrastructure(s), social meaning(s), and social capital(s) necessary for the urban revitalization and environmental restoration of our cities?

• How can green infrastructure be designed to contribute to the resilience of social communities and ecological processes?

(For color images and illustrations, go to http://beslter.org/social_mosaics.)

References

Bell, W. 1997. Foundations of Futures Studies: Human Science for a New Era. New Brunswick: Transaction Publishers.

Berkes, F. and C. Folke, editors. 2000. Linking Social and Ecological Systems: Management Practices and Social Mechanisms for building Building Resilience. New York: Cambridge University Press.

Bormann, F.H. and G. Likens. 1979. Patterns and Processes in a Forested Ecosystem. New York: Springer-Verlag.

Burch, W.R. 1988. Human Ecology and Environmental Management. In: Agee, J. K., and R. J. Darryll, editors. Ecosystem Management for Parks and Wilderness. Seattle: University of Washington Press. pp. 145-159.

Garreau, J. 1991. Edge City: Life on the New Frontier. New York: Doubleday.

Glickman, L.B. 1999. Bibliographic Essay. In Glickman, L.B., editor. Consumer Society in American History: A Reader. Ithaca: Cornell University Press. pp. 399-414.

Gottdiener, M. and R. Hutchinson. 2001. The New Urban Sociology. New York: McGraw-Hill Higher Education.

Groffman, P.M., D.J. Bain, et al. 2003. Down by the Riverside: Urban Riparian Ecology. Journal of Environmental Ecology 1(6): 315-321.

Grove, J.M., W. R. Burch and S.T.A. Pickett. 2005. Social Mosaics and Urban Forestry in Baltimore, Maryland. Pp. 248-273. In Communities and Forests: Where People Meet the Land, edited by R. G. Lee and D. R. Field. Corvalis: Oregon State University Press.

Halter, M. 2000. Shopping for Identity: the Marketing of Ethnicity. New York: Schocken Books.

Horowitz, D. 1985. The Morality of Spending: Attitudes towards the Consumer Society in America, 1876-1940. Baltimore: Johns Hopkins University Press.

Hough, M. 1984. City Form and Natural Process: Towards a New Uurban Vernacular. New York: Van Nostrand Reinhold Company.

Katz, B. and J. Bradley. (1999). Divided We Sprawl. Atlantic Monthly (284): 26-42.

Keller, E.B., J.L. Berry, et al. 2003. The Influentials: One American in Ten Tells the Other Nine How to Vote, Where to Eat, and What to Buy. New York: Free Press.

MEANING

BLOCKS + ALLEYS
PERCEPTUAL BOUNDARIES

NOCTURNAL EMISSIONS

LIGHT SIGNATURE

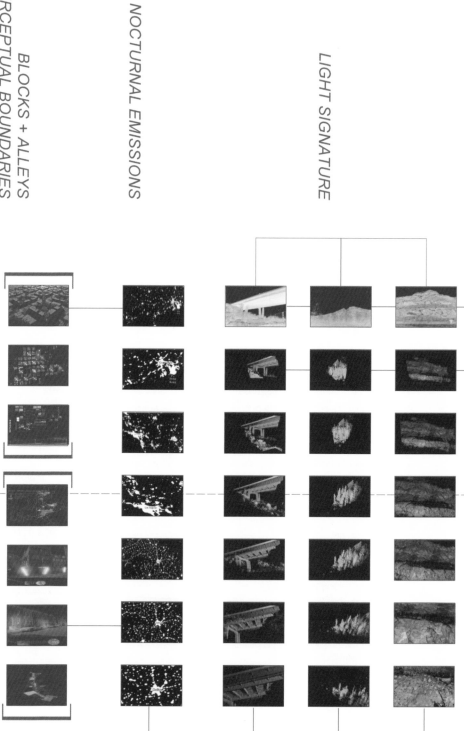

POINT CLOUD

MIXING SPACE

SHIFTING MOSAIC

THREAD C:
LIGHT NETWORKS

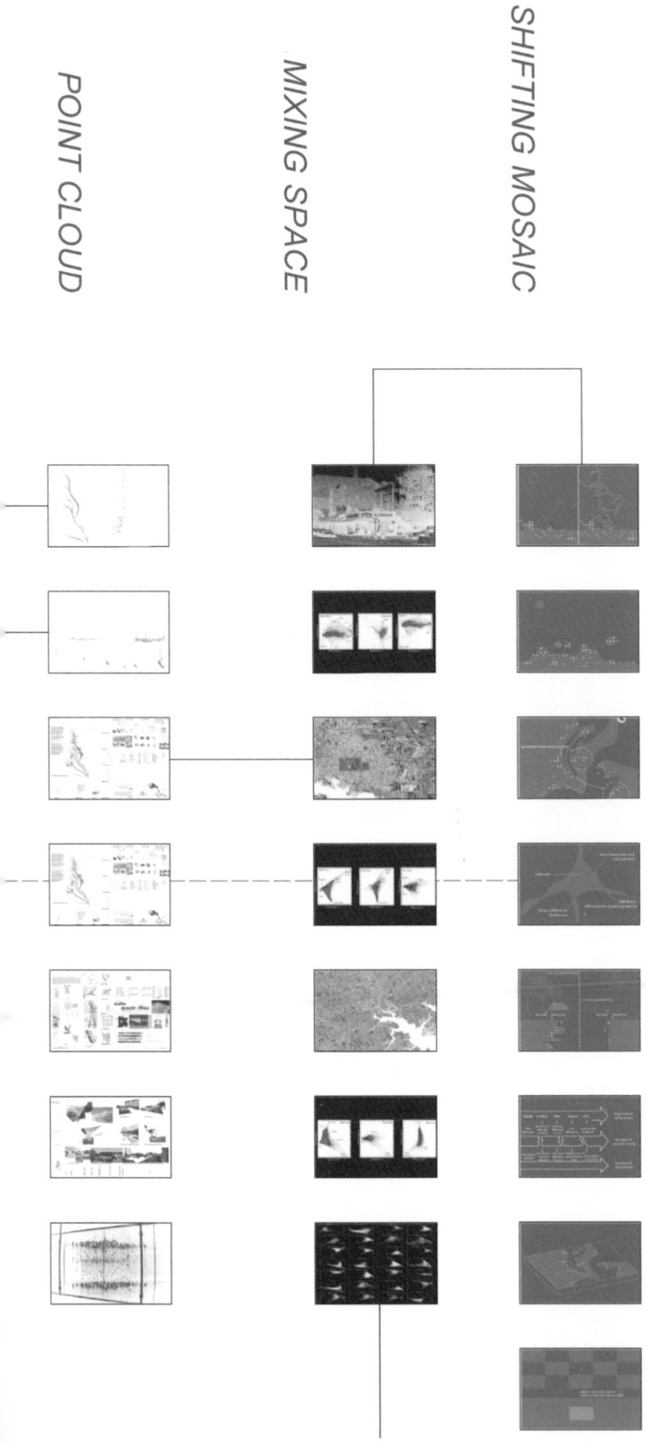

URBAN DESIGN STUDENT WORK 2003, WATERSHED 263.
Victoria Marshall, Brian McGrath, Joel Towers, Critics.

Manhattan Ground Level Digital Photo
Christopher Small, 2004

Color images containing multiple color layers can be
visualized geometrically within spectral mixing spaces.
Multidimensional mixing spaces reveal structure and
properties not readily apperent in the spatial format of
the image. A ground level digital photo of a Manhattan
street scene can be represented as a 3 dimensional density cloud in which each pixel in the image occupies a location within the cloud corresponding to the red, green
and blue brightness values of the pixel. The 3D structure
of the cloud can be visualized using a series of orthogo-
nal 2D projections of the cloud. Because many pixels can
have the same color (hence the same 3D coordinates),
the density of the cloud varies in accordance with the
frequency of different color pixels in the image. In the
mixing space projections, the warmer colors indicate
denser regions within the cloud. The top row of mixing
space projections corresponds to the street scene image
where different color objects result in distinct clusters
within the cloud.

Infrared satellite images can also be visualized with mixing spaces. Comparisons of spectral mixing spaces of
urban areas worldwide reveal a consistent tetrahedral
structure in which the spectral properties of the urban
mosaic can be represented as linear mixtures of vegetation, soils, bright substrates, water, shadow and dark
absorptive surfaces. The mixing spaces in the center and
bottom rows correspond to visible/infrared images of
New York City at neighborhood and regional scales (re-
spectively) and have a similar topology to other cities
worldwide. Additional mixing spaces and infrared imagery of numerous cities worldwide are available online at:
http://www.ldeo.columbia.edu/~small/Urban.html

Manhattan Ground Level Digital Photo:
Mixing Space (opposite)
Christopher Small, 2004

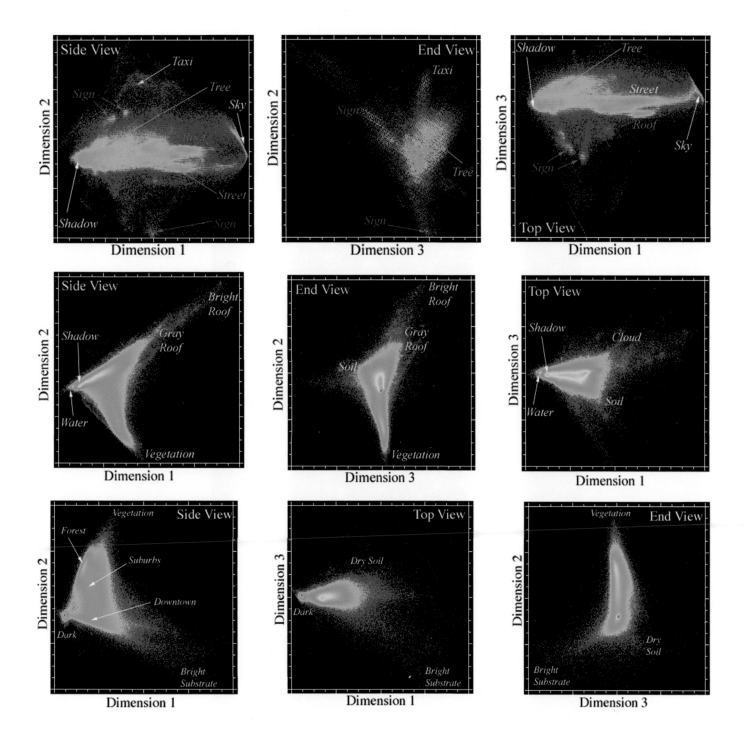

Light Composite
Christopher Small, 2004

Night lights provide an alternative depiction of human population distribution at global scales. Sensors imaging nocturnal emissions in the visible and near infrared provide globally consistent representations of lighted human settlements. At 1 km pixel resolution almost all moderate to large settlement are resolved and provide greater spatial detail than population censuses in most developing and some developed countries. Comparing night lighting at different times provides a means of mapping changes in lighted extent as indicated by the temporal color key in the images below.

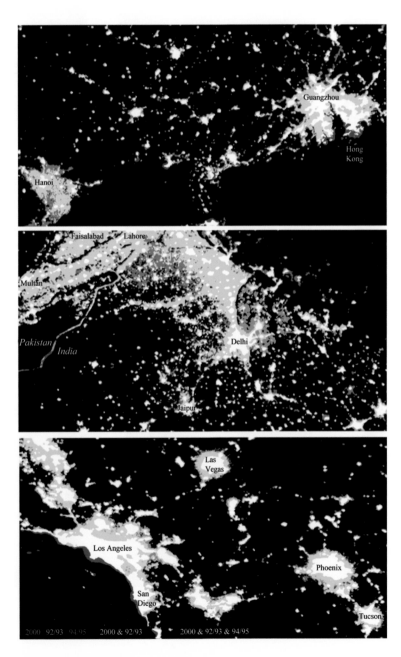

Unbounding Communities

Nicolas Bacigalupo, Vivian Hernandez, Tim Reed, Keunsook Suk, Van Tsing Hung, 2003

This project uses perceptual boundaries as an urban design tool. This is achieved by linking neighborhoods together, capitalizing on their inherent social patterns toward forming more variable collectivities along an armature. Breaking of perceptual borders can open the residents of the watershed to rethink what their physical environment is and can be. To begin this process we provide identities using specific iconographic elements such as lighting, water retention, and memory; giving each their own iconography. The iconography serves as a visual connection and a way finding device. In addition, the armature provides a focus for reinvestment and improved public health.

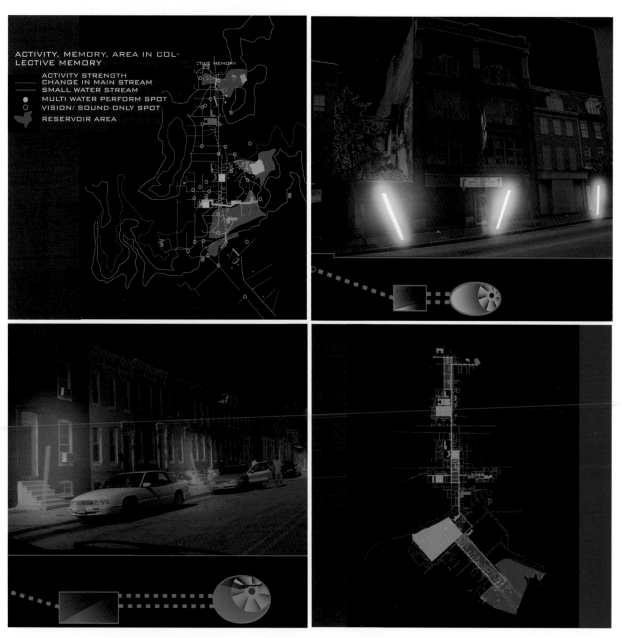

Using methods of range scanning, registering and texture mapping, this project aimed to reproduce photo realistic models of certain landscapes and infrastructural features that exist in the area that lies within the vicinity of the upcoming Allied Junction Transfer station in Secaucus, New Jersey. While the project was not completed as planned, the resulting images revealed their potential as an urban design tool.

Snake Hill/3D Camera: Point Cloud Bridge
Peter Allen, Paul Blaer, Andrew Brotzman,
Pavi Sriprakash, 2002

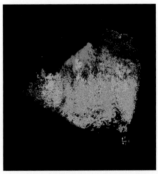

Snake Hill/3D Camera: Point Cloud Trees
Peter Allen, Paul Blaer, Andrew Brotzman,
Pavi Sriprakash, and Jiang Zhu, 2002

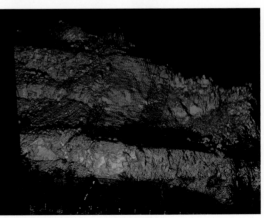

**Snake Hill/3D Camera: Point Cloud Rocks with
Texture Map**
Peter Allen, Paul Blaer, Andrew Brotzman,
Pavi Sriprakash, and Jiang Zhu, 2002

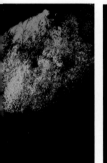

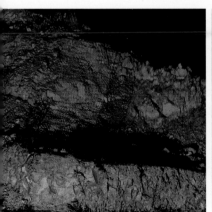

Trashcape

Oliver Valle, Esi-Kilanga Ifeytayo Bowser, Joseph Plouffe,
Kim DeFreitas, 2003

The intention of this project is to understand the various
conditions within boundaries at the neighborhood scale
based on the hypothetical model of patch dynamics using trash as a dynamic filter.

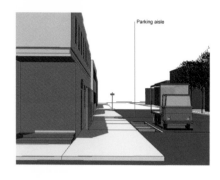

Parking aisle

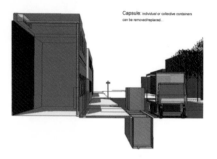

Capsule: individual or collective containers can be removed/replaced...

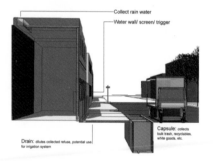

Collect rain water

Water wall/ screen/ trigger

Drain: dilutes collected refuse, potential use for irrigation system

Capsule: collects bulk trash, recyclables, white goods, etc.

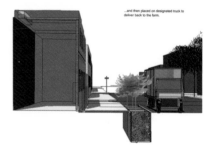

...and then placed on designated truck to deliver back to the farm.

Double Section
Flora Hsiang-I Chen, 2003

Spring Condition A

Autumn Condition A

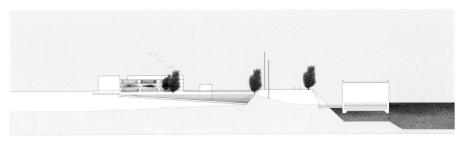

Autumn Condition B

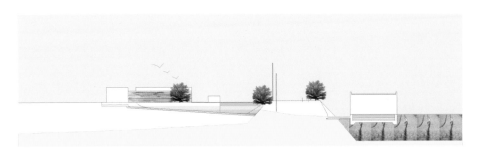

Spring Condition B

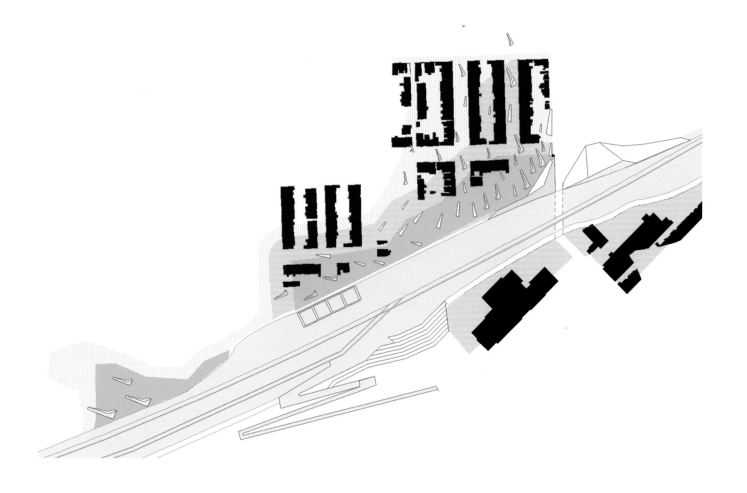

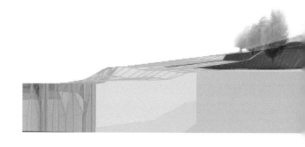

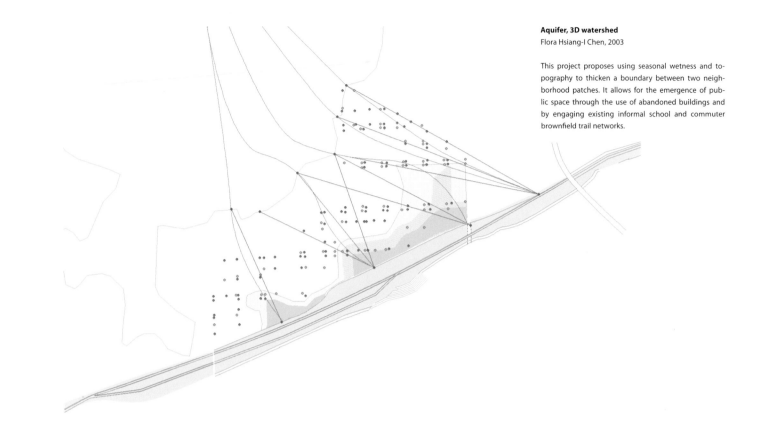

Aquifer, 3D watershed
Flora Hsiang-I Chen, 2003

This project proposes using seasonal wetness and topography to thicken a boundary between two neighborhood patches. It allows for the emergence of public space through the use of abandoned buildings and by engaging existing informal school and commuter brownfield trail networks.

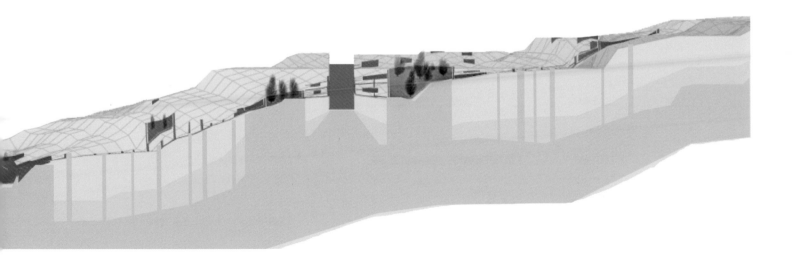

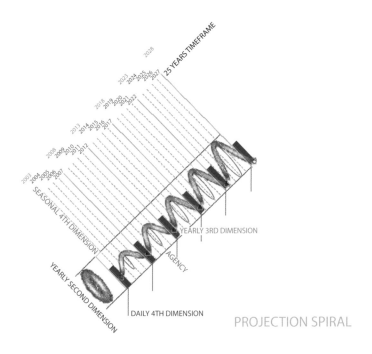

2028
2023 2024 2025 2026 2027 25 YEARS TIMEFRAME
2018 2019 2020 2021 2022
2013 2014 2015 2016 2017
2008 2009 2010 2011 2012
2003 2004 2005 2006 2007

SEASONAL 4TH DIMENSION

YEARLY SECOND DIMENSION

YEARLY 3RD DIMENSION

AGENCY

DAILY 4TH DIMENSION

PROJECTION SPIRAL

Temporal Filters Timeline
Joseph Plouffe, Jenny Jie Zhou, Derek Mizner, Kim
DeFreitas, Chin-Hua Huang, 2003

SEASONAL TIMELINE / EVERCHANGING AGENCY

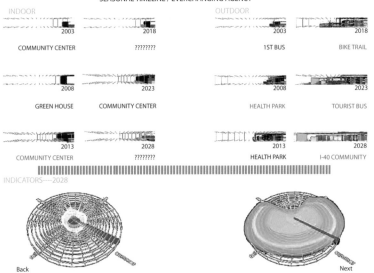

INDOOR

2003	2018
COMMUNITY CENTER	????????
2008	2023
GREEN HOUSE	COMMUNITY CENTER
2013	2028
COMMUNITY CENTER	????????

OUTDOOR

2003	2018
1ST BUS	BIKE TRAIL
2008	2023
HEALTH PARK	TOURIST BUS
2013	2028
HEALTH PARK	I-40 COMMUNITY

INDICATORS----2028

Back   Next

Temporal Filters Season
Joseph Plouffe, Jenny Jie Zhou, Derek Mizner, Kim
DeFreitas, Chin-Hua Huang, 2003

Temporal Filters Spiral

Joseph Plouffe, Jenny Jie Zhou, Derek Mizner, Kim DeFreitas, Chin-Hua Huang, 2003

This project proposes a spiral time framework as an urban design model to engage the watershed residents to consolidate the dispersed resources of the neighborhood.

Instead of fixing our field of view in certain solid time-space, the students project a 25-year time frame and highlight the traces of the transformation as a repetitive and ever-changing sequence of programming.

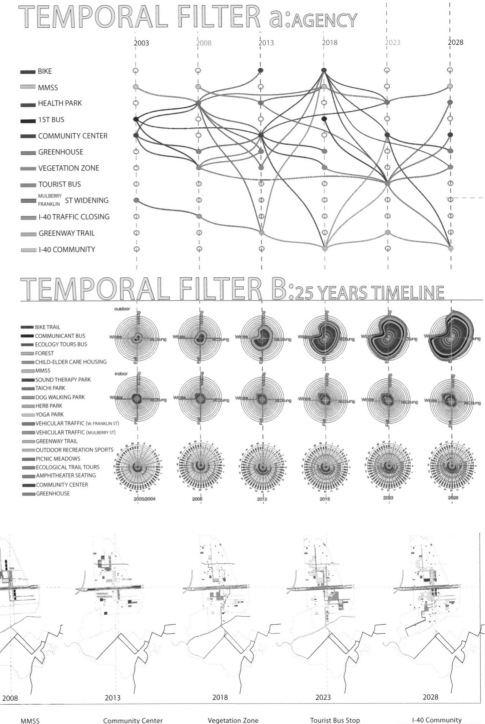

TEMPORAL FILTER a:AGENCY

2003   2008   2013   2018   2023   2028

- BIKE
- MMSS
- HEALTH PARK
- 1ST BUS
- COMMUNITY CENTER
- GREENHOUSE
- VEGETATION ZONE
- TOURIST BUS
- MULBERRY FRANKLIN ST WIDENING
- I-40 TRAFFIC CLOSING
- GREENWAY TRAIL
- I-40 COMMUNITY

TEMPORAL FILTER B:25 YEARS TIMELINE

- BIKE TRAIL
- COMMUNICANT BUS
- ECOLOGY TOURS BUS
- FOREST
- CHILD-ELDER CARE HOUSING
- MMSS
- SOUND THERAPY PARK
- TAICHI PARK
- DOG WALKING PARK
- HERB PARK
- YOGA PARK
- VEHICULAR TRAFFIC (W. FRANKLIN ST)
- VEHICULAR TRAFFIC (MULBERRY ST)
- GREENWAY TRAIL
- OUTDOOR RECREATION SPORTS
- PICNIC MEADOWS
- ECOLOGICAL TRAIL TOURS
- AMPHITHEATER SEATING
- COMMUNITY CENTER
- GREENHOUSE

2003/2004   2008   2013   2018   2023   2028

2003/2004   2008   2013   2018   2023   2028

PROJECTION

Mulberry Franklin St Widening   MMSS   Community Center   Vegetation Zone   Tourist Bus Stop   I-40 Community

CHAPTER IV

URBAN PATCHES: GRANULATION, PATTERNS AND PATCHWORKS

GRAHAME SHANE

Urban Patch Formation

The dictionary defines a patch as "patch, piece of cloth, metal, etc., put on to mend a whole or rent... large or irregular spot on a surface; piece of ground; number of plants growing on this, as a patch of beans" (The Concise Oxford Dictionary 1937). A patch is a distinct, bounded entity or surface, a piece of material or land that covers or connects with the surrounding pieces to form a larger network, a patchwork. The meaning of patchwork is "a work made of various cloths sewn together; (fig) work of uneven quality; jumble; rough mixture."

From these definitions it follows that urban patches are distinct entities whose relationships with their neighbors are very important. Without these linkages and bonds the entire system would collapse. As distinct entities, like enclaves, they have more or less porous boundaries and a consistent texture controlled by codes that are set by the dominant urban actor within the patch. Urban "actors" are land owners, merchants at a fair, priests in a church, legal authorities in a court, political representatives, the occupants of the patch themselves, or perhaps a negotiated intermediary social entity among all these parties.

Patches stand as discrete areas of order with their own internal system of self-organization in which feedback loops reinforce the dominant code, setting the normative structure. Actors impose systems of organization within their patch to create order, increasing the entropy outside. These systems reflect habitual, repetitive, social relationships and hierarchies of value within a community in a particular patch or place. Actors may employ physical force, intimidation or exclusionary tactics if necessary, thus setting up heterotopias - the place of the "other"- as holding pens for those excluded.

A single owner or multiple occupants can make and control a patch, but in any case the idea of a patchwork implies that each patch is part of a larger system. The multiple connections to neighbors ensure that shifting relationships will develop with other patches. Actors responding to perturbations or disturbances in their larger urban system can tailor their piece of the patchwork to take advantage of the larger system's dynamics. Urban patches involve creating structures for multiple occupants to share in a local situation and depend for their success on the accommodation of disparate actors. Such structures can be impermanent, and they can occur almost anywhere that is convenient in a variable network of trade or flows.

Janet Abu-Lughod, in *Before European Hegemony: The World System AD 1250-1350*, begins with a study of "A System in Formation," describing in general terms how a city might evolve around a temporary market to service a settled, agricultural economy that could afford luxuries. Abu-Lughod shows how these temporary market day structures could become linked for merchants who traveled in a weekly loop. From these transitory beginnings, the market day structures transformed over time into permanent events, like the medieval trade fairs of Flanders, which linked into global systems (Abu-Lughod 1989).

In the case of Flanders, these links included local connections to Northern Italy and the Mediterranean trading-basin, with long distance linkages stretching across the Middle East and Central Asia to India and China. The Flanders fairs lasted a hundred years and became institutionalized in great market halls. Then the fairs faded from view for 100 years after the plague of the Black Death, carried by fleas from Asia, killed a third of Europe's population in the 1350s.

Abu-Lughod depicts this early version of a global trade system with patches of urbanity at crucial node points, anticipating the later colonial and industrial schemes of the European powers from the 16th to 19th centuries. Her description is based on Immanuel Wallerstein's World Systems theories of the 1970s that began to map the emergence of the post-colonial global hierarchies of cities serving as urban nodes or patches inside an emerging, complex, accelerated, mediated network of communication and transportation (Wallerstein 1974).

Patches created by urban actors in the 1250s in Europe or Asia are obviously very different from patches that developed during the Industrial Revolution in Britain in the 1780s, where multi-story factories and workers' cottages might stand isolated in the countryside beside a canal. The network supporting a small urban industrial patch like Wedgwood's Etruria Pottery Works in Staffordshire, England is clearly dissimilar to the vast steel mills of the later monopoly-capitalists such as Andrew Carnegie's U.S. Steel Corporation in Pittsburgh, and distinct again from Steve Jobs' Apple campus in Cupertino, California in Silicon Valley.

Urban Patches and Urban Grain

Patches can vary enormously in design, scale, function and form. Within a patch a set of actors creates a distinctive urban grain to house their activities in a particular area. The dictionary defines a grain as "a seed or fruit that can be used as food, a small particle or crystal…the stratification of fibers in wood due to pressure or texture in stone due to constituent particles or fibers." The term stratification, or layering, is especially important here. "Granules" are derived from the noun grain, as is the verb granulation, meaning to form into grains or crystals.

The grain of the city and urban granulation are specialized terms used by urban historians and designers to designate a particular pattern of settlement organization and process of urbanization created in a specific place and time. Urban granulation implies that urban actors perform as catalysts under pressure, searching for an emerging order and creating fixed structures from the chaotic, nomadic situation associated with trade networks and flows. Actors' choices crystallize the urban grain as a layer reflecting the pressure of a wider economic, social, and temporal network of relationships. Such decisions are often made in response to disturbances in the system. The patterns of organization and various grains reflect the actors' cultural values and show how they handle the many forces in their environment. Actors' choices become encoded over time as local, vernacular building traditions, linked to economic needs, transport technologies, and communications networks.

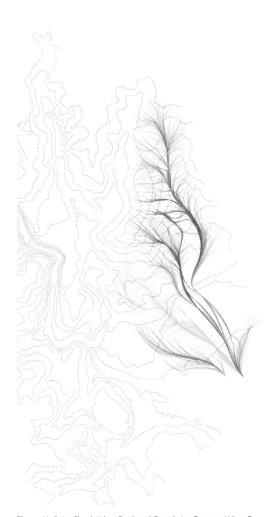

Figure 40. Point Cloud, Urban Patch and Granulation Patterns: Urban Contours and Stream Paths/ Flows.

Kevin Lynch, in *The Image of the City* (1961), highlighted the difference between the existing downtown grain of Boston's North End and the new flow space of surrounding the Central Artery, a raised, regional highway bisecting the city. Lynch was interested in how local inhabitants mapped their city using the concept of urban grain. Like Jane Jacobs in *The Life and Death of Great American Cities* (1960), Lynch contrasted small-scale, self-organizing, communal city elements of the old city with large-scale, modern, rationalist elements (Lynch 1960).

Concurrently, the term "urban grain" reappeared as the Cornell Contextualists, lead by Colin Rowe, turned back to Camillo Sitte in order to critique Le Corbusier's modern town planning practices. Sitte's *City Planning According to Artistic Principles* (1899) argued that most churches, palaces and public buildings of Medieval and Renaissance cities were normally buried in the urban fabric surrounding the public piazzas. He contrasted the close-packed fabric of the medieval city with the wide open spaces of the modern Vienna Ringstrasse. He developed a stark, high contrast, "figure-ground" drawing technique that articulated the grain of the buildings in black in contrast to the public open spaces in white.

Lynch went beyond Sitte by assigning each grain of the city a code that allowed the bonding of varied uses in different ways. The small scale, self-organizing system allowed mixed use at a small scale and was termed "fine grain". Lynch named as "coarse grain" large-scale units of organization that tended to be mono-functional elements in the city, such as a modernist housing complex.

Each urban grain also had a time signature associating it with a "fast" or a "slow" system of transportation and communication. For Lynch, the Italian immigrant community in the historic North End of Boston belonged to a slow system and inhabited a fine-grained, small-scale pattern of urbanization facilitating self-organization and organic community development. The highway cut across this community and was part of a coarse grain system serving the suburbs and working at an entirely different speed and scale. Lynch also recognized the landscape dimension of the automo-

Figure 41. Urban Grain Watershed 263, 1936, Urban Patch and Granulation Patterns; Colonial Grid Settlement (inside red frame) and 19th Century City Extension ignore stream paths and topography; Industrial port district distinct.

Figure 42. Urban Grain Watershed 263, 2002. Urban Patch and Granulation patterns. Erosion of 19th Century Grid by automobile (highway, move to suburbs and abandonment along stream paths).

bile city, searching for patterns in suburban developments at a new vast scale of a city "territory" (Lynch 1961).

Urban Patches and Urban Patterns

Before the advent of the automobile, urban historians and designers had archived the many different patterns and formations of urban grain over the centuries. These patterns are categorized as urban morphologies, a term derived from the Greek "logos," meaning study or logic, and "morphos," meaning shape. The study of shape or the logic of combinations dates back hundreds of years.

The Greeks used the five Platonic solids as a basic geometrical language of shapes. Their theory of city building evolved through debating the ideal plan, the ideal constitution, the role of public space (the agora) and the use of the grid in colonies. For the Greeks, and later Romans, an important determinant of the shape of a city was the "topos," i.e. the place and local factors like contour, site orientation, availability of water or a harbor, etc.

Urban morphologists have studied these global patterns, each in their own trading network and continent, with their own sets of values and peculiar forms adjusted to their climate, needs, and times. We can easily make basic distinctions in building form and urban pattern from continent to continent, culture to culture. Courtyard house types, for instance, were common in Greek and Roman Classical cultures, and continued to be used in Chinese, Indian, and Arabic cultures until the 20th century. Similarly the descendants of the Vikings and other northern settlers preferred linear arrangements of long houses, row houses, merchant shop houses, and streets, resulting in the row house typology that also continued into the 20th century. Both systems were supplemented by industrial inventions like large sheds for factories, skyscrapers, and modern slab and tower blocks for residential and commercial uses.

Anne Vernez Moudon argues that European morphologists, with their static series of types and fixed forms descended from Plato, cannot account for the systematic changes over time and that a new system of "morphogenesis" is necessary to track changes of shape and formal structures in social use over time. In making this argument, Moudon outlines the three dominant morphological schools of the past century, which are based in England, France and Italy (Moudon 1994).

The British School, founded by M.R. Conzens in the 1930s, emphasized the cadastral or land subdivision system that lay below the building types, linking into English property ownership legal records for evidence of urban evolution. The Italian School, based in Venice and also dating from the 1930s, emphasized the Rationalist logic of construction starting from the room, and building up through the stair, house, courtyard, row house, etc. to develop a systematic study of the urban fabric, concluding with the open spaces between buildings. The Versailles-based French School of the 1960s pioneered the combination of these two methodologies by joining the study of built form patterns with land ownership patterns in the Royal French new town of Versailles from the 1660s onwards.

The Versailles studies showed the shift from the street and square system based on row houses for royal functionaries to a system of villas in gardens for aristocrats, reflecting the values of the crown with their vast new palace facing the gardens. This change anticipated a larger cultural shift in the 19th century when the middle class bourgeoisie of Europe sought refuge from the Industrial Revolution in peripheral garden suburbs, initiating what Paola Vigano in *La Città Elementare* (1999) calls the "Reverse City" set in the landscape (Vigano 1999).

Lynch's *Good City Form* (1961) also offered urban designers and city planners tools for modeling the expanded patterns of the city based on automobiles. He provided a system for the notation of urban characteristics that could be scaled up from the pedestrian to the automobile city region. Lynch's notation consisted of urban patches with special characteristics indicated by cross hatching, diagonal stripes, or dots. Corridors or paths of movement had their own characteristics, denoted by dotted, dashed, or solid lines (Lynch 1961).

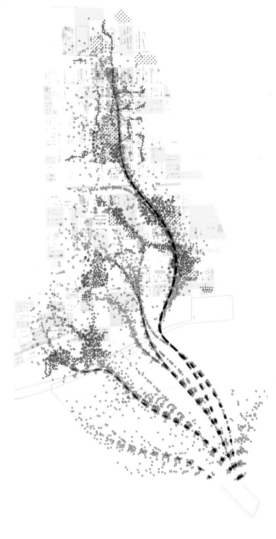

Figure 43. Urban Patch and Granulation Patterns; Interaction of urban granulation and Stream Paths.

Urban patches could be arrayed in different formations. Patches could converge upon a single center or on multiple nodes in ring and radial patterns. Lynch posited three "normative" urban models - the City of Faith, the City as a Machine and the Organic City - each with its own arrangement of patches. The pattern could shift from a single center (City of Faith) to tension between two centers of attraction such as center and edge or old and new (the City as Machine). From this bi-polar linear system, a multi-centered city of satellite patches (the Organic City) could develop that Lynch modeled in various ways as the Patchwork City, the Galaxy City and the Polycentric City diagrams.

Urban Patches: Ecologies and Patch Dynamics

Lynch's polycentric models took on a new interest in the 1990s as satellite imagery of global megacities like Mexico City, Mumbai or Lagos appeared on morphologists' monitors. In the Second World War, aerial reconnaissance photography and analysis allowed urban actors to distinguish different urban patches as targets and later aided in assessing damage from bombing raids. Modernists employed such photos to outline areas for slum clearance. Ecologists and urban planners rebuilding Germany used aerial photos to analyze urban patches as part of a wider network system with patches of forest and agriculture interspersed with settlements.

Urban geographer Walter Christaller was amongst these pioneers and went on to mathematically model the multi-centered hierarchies of the Dutch "Ring City" as a network. Christaller, like the Modernists, envisioned a network of cities in which modern transportation and communications created an even playing field and homogeneous space. The Swedish Government, neutral during the Second World War, applied this theory in its new town policy. The post-war government was puzzled by their failure, which was investigated by Torsten Hägerstrand, urban planner of Lund University in the 1950s (Hall 1988) (Buttimer 1983).

Hägerstrand advised the Swedish Government to invest in specialized uses in each town. This differentiation and specialization set in motion the catalytic processes of urban actors who could then exploit small differences and niche opportunities, setting up shifting relationships among the towns and bringing them to life.

Hägerstrand also hypothesized that with modern communications people would have wider networks of contacts and therefore need more places to meet and interact, urban patches that he called "milieu," a French term meaning local network or atmosphere. Later, Hägerstrand's theories, calculations, and mathematical models served as the basis for marketing consultants planning mall locations for developers in the expanding American suburbs.

Ecologists employed similar mathematical models of flows and patches in their studies of flora, fauna, flows, boundary environments, and patches to develop sophisticated mathematical models of patches and their interactions known as Patch Dynamics. From the 1980s onwards, ecologists used these models to make simulations of their proposed interventions and calculate the most favorable environmental solution according to given parameters (Dramstad, Olson, Forman 1996). Satellite imagery in the 1990s and Geographical Information Systems (G.I.S.) in the 2000s have allowed urban ecologists to model their patches in real time. The USDA Forest Service, for instance, is currently mapping the Urban Forests of the United States East Coast using satellite imagery supplemented by land and tax records, in an effort to assess the potential to influence climate change (Svendsen, Marshall and Ufer 2005).

Conclusion: The need for a morphogenesis of patches and patchworks

Moudon's focus on morphogenesis, including the time element of the city rather than the static forms of morphology, became especially important as aerial night satellite photography from the early 21st century made the self-organizing network characteristics of this global urban system of patches especially clear on a daily and monthly basis. Morphologists in the past worked at a microscopic scale based on a rationalist analysis of plot, house type, the relationship to the street and public space, the disposition of larger-scale public institutions and parks, etc. They emphasized the construction of the patch as city fabric; its patterns, iterative structures, codes and traditions.

Morphogenetic analysis stresses the time element of an urban actor's choices that are specific to a particular place, culture and set of flows in local and global networks. This approach can include multiple scales and time frames. Forms that were built at one time for one purpose may lie redundant for a period and then become re-inhabited in unexpected ways. Also, a patchwork city may contain multiple actors who may simultaneously create very different structures reflecting their understanding of flows, their position in a network of relationships and their preferences (in Lynch's terms) for a fast or slow fabric with a fine or course grain.

The great advantage of the morphogenetic approach is that it allows the analysis of patches in time and the spaces in-between them as well, including the landscape, "terrain vague", and lost or interstitial spaces often neglected in morphological studies. This emphasis creates a model that, like a sponge, has both a system of fabric and system of voids, each with their own time dimension. The sponge metaphor fits a patchwork city that is layered in a three dimensional matrix, containing an interwoven network of patches and voids, each with its own code of internal and external relationships, sets of values and time frame. Advanced communications and transportation systems tie all these patches and voids together to create Vigano's "Reverse City" territory with its intervals and dynamics of spacing.

The morphogenetic approach can also include those excluded spaces of the "other" - the heterotopias that help stabilize each system by accommodating actors in a state of crisis, confronting a disturbance in their life and needing a flexible, hybrid, multi-cellular structure to allow experimentation and change. Actors may hide these structures in patches inside a city, place them outside in isolation on the periphery, or distribute them widely across the advanced communication network. Examples might include a hidden, forbidden Catholic chapel in a Dutch townhouse in Protestant Amsterdam; a panopticon jail with its stacked cells around an invisible central jailer on the edge of an industrial town; or a multi-level mall in a suburban ring with multiple centers, connected to global suppliers.

The morphogenetic approach also allows the mapping of building and city transformations and re-combinations over time. All the above examples are multi-layered, sectional complexes that compress and accelerate change in miniature patches, mirroring and altering the dominant codes of the contemporary city. Here we can see that urban actors are simultaneously employing several systems and models of urbanization layered on each other in a complicated patchwork that is linked to global networks. In such complexes actors can model and experiment with a new kind of system of self-organization that we are only just beginning to understand.

We live in an age of global, mass urbanization on an unprecedented scale. We have only just begun to model the world system in terms of a complex mechanism that sorts and ranks patches, feeding on a shifting set of power relations left over from the previous colonial regimes. Meanwhile, our cities form strange new patchworks composed of ancient urban forms, vast industrial complexes, business centers, mega-malls and giant barrios of self-built housing juxtaposed in close proximity. A patch-based, three-dimensional ecological and morphogenetic approach could greatly facilitate our studies.

References

The Concise Oxford Dictionary. 1937. Oxford: OUP. Third Edition.

Anne Buttimer, ed. 1983. Creativity and Context, Lund Studies in Geography #50. Lund:Royal University of Lund, Dept of Geography.

Abu-Lughod, Janet. 1989. Before European Hegemony: The World System A.D. 1250-1350. New York: Oxford University Press. Chapter 1.

W. Dramstad, J.D. Olson, R.T.T. Forman. 1996. Landscape Ecology Principles in Landscape Architecture and Land-Use Planning. Harvard University Press. p 19-25.

Hall, Peter. 1988. Cities of Tomorrow: An Intellectual History of Town Urban Planning and Design in the Twentieth Century, Oxford: Blackwell. p 327.

Lynch, Kevin. 1961. Good City Form. Cambridge, Mass: MIT Press. p 81, 148-149.

Lynch, Kevin. 1960. The Image of the City. Cambridge, Mass: Technology Press. p 16-32.

Moudon, Anne Vernez. 1994. Getting to Know the Built Landscape: Typomorphology. In Ordering Space: Types in Architectural Design, Karen Franck and Lynda H. Schneekloth (eds). New York: Van Nostrand Reinholt. p 289-311.

E. Svendsen, V. Marshall and M. Ufer. 2005. Urban Field Guide Baltimore Maryland in McGrath and Shane (eds).Sensing the 21st Century City: Close-up and remote, AD Special Issue. London:Wiley-Academy. p 26-31.

Sitte, Camillo. 1986. City Planning According to Artistic Principles. 1899. in G.R. Collins and C.C. Collins, Camillo Sitte:The Birth of Modern City Planning. New York: Rizzoli.

Vigano, Paola. 1999. La Città Elementare. Milan: Skira. p 88.

Wallerstein, Immanuel. 1974. The Modern World System - Capitalist Agriculture and the Origins of the European World-Economy in the Sixteenth Century. New York: Academy Press.

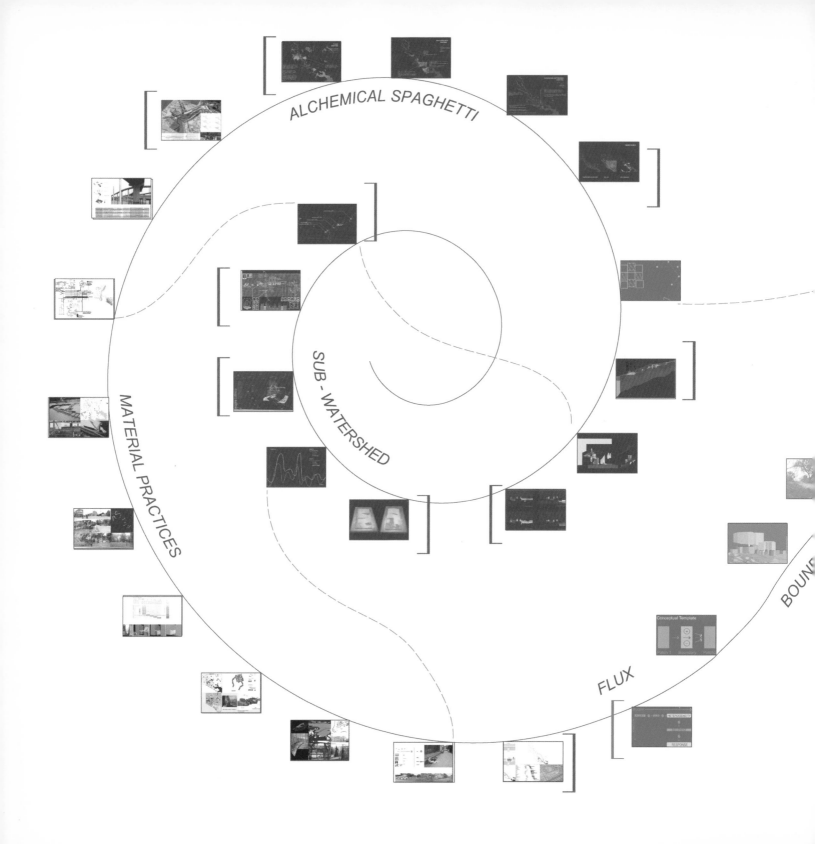

ALCHEMICAL SPAGHETTI

SUB - WATERSHED

MATERIAL PRACTICES

FLUX

BOUND

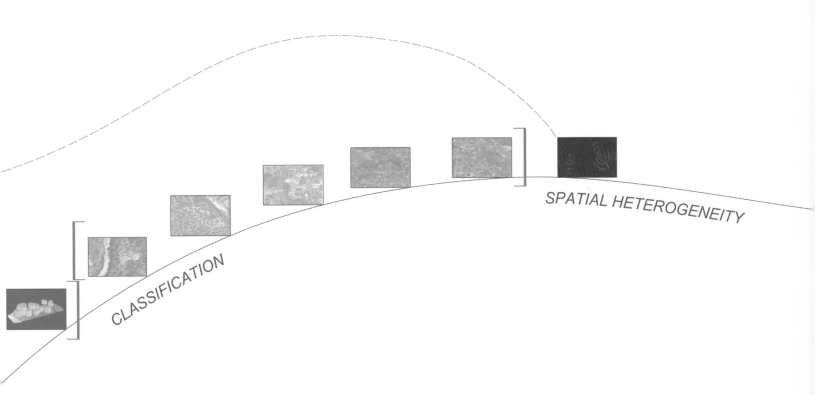

CLASSIFICATION

SPATIAL HETEROGENEITY

THREAD D:
SPIRAL LANDSCAPES

Urban System Classification
Class Components

Building
   Single sturctures arrayed
   in rows or clusters
Connected structures
   Parking type
   Presence of parking lots
   Absence of parking lots
Vegetation
   Coarse vegetation at low density
   Coarse vegetation at medium density
   Coarse vegetation at high density

"Using this new classification scheme has allowed us to quantify the structure of different neighborhoods in the Gwynns Falls watershed. We can determine how the neighborhoods differ from each other in terms of the types of classes present and the relative proportion of land area that each class type occupies. We plan to apply this classification to the entire Gwynns Falls watershed and we anticipate acquiring imagery of the Gwynns Falls every 5 years so that we can determine how the structures of different areas in the watershed are changing"

~Mary Cadenasso. October, 2003. 'Baltimore Ecosystem Study Community Open House'

Gwynns Falls Boundary Classification
Example I, Gwynns Falls, Baltimore
Mary Cadenasso, 2002

Gwynns Falls Boudary Classification
Example II, Gwynns Falls, Baltimore
Mary Cadenasso, 2002

Gwynns Falls Boudary Classification
Example III, Gwynns Falls, Baltimore
Mary Cadenasso, 2002

Gwynns Falls Boudary Classification
Example IV, Gwynns Falls, Baltimore
Mary Cadenasso, 2002

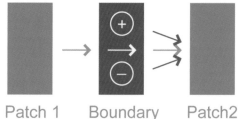

Conceptual Template

Patch 1   Boundary   Patch2

Crown Structure Photo
M.L. Cadenasso, 2002

Boundary Location: South Africa
M.L. Cadenasso, 2003

Conceptual Template
M.L. Cadenasso, 2002

South Africa 3D Patch
M.L. Cadenasso, 2002

Image set of linked tools of framework, model template, and working model with an experimental study of field-river edge boundary function.

URBAN DESIGN STUDENT WORK 2003, WATERSHED 263.
Victoria Marshall, Brian McGrath, Joel Towers, Critics.

Urban Imbrications (opposite)
Gurpreet Shah, Poku Chen, Amit Talwar, Emilia Ferri, and Peter Robinson, 2003

"The long term reproduction of a neighborhood that is simultaneously practical, valued and taken for granted depends on the seamless interaction of localized spaces and times with local subjects possessed of the knowledge to reproduce locality."   -Arjun Appadurai.

The project situates itself as a network of interference in which systems of program, nodes and alleys interplay to articulate previously hidden zones of potential occupation within the existing fabric of the Baltimore watershed.

Alleys reveal connectivity and challenge the definition of use/non-use as part of a system of familial connections that dissolve and interweave the edges of neighborhoods and abandoned patches of vacant space within the watershed. This alley system of secret and apparent negotiations support (by physical connections) a real vision for a twenty-five year growth pattern.

Blocks and alleys are restructured with the use of different color lighting on the corners of vacant lots creating towers of light and a sense of cohesiveness yet diversity throughout the neighborhoods. This results in a neighborhood fabric that resembles a de Stijl canvas and allows for a system of program to be located within the vacant sites and connect via the alley system.

Following the 25-year timeline the program system of renewable energy and urban agriculture moves from a closed system in which previously abandoned spaces are imagined as self-contained, self-energized zones accessed through the alley system. Over time these program areas grow into an extended system of shared resources and ultimately to a regional system where resources simultaneously operate as closed and extended systems within the watershed.

The resultant project illustrates the interplay of these various elements in reifying a new way of viewing the Baltimore watershed. That which has been discarded as blight is now an integral part of a self-sustaining energy and familial network. Secret paths through the alleys and cracks within the row house typology unveil sites of programmed occupation. Through the integral self-sustained energy produced at these sites a constellation of light towers illuminate the night sky and give visceral presence to the Baltimore watershed.

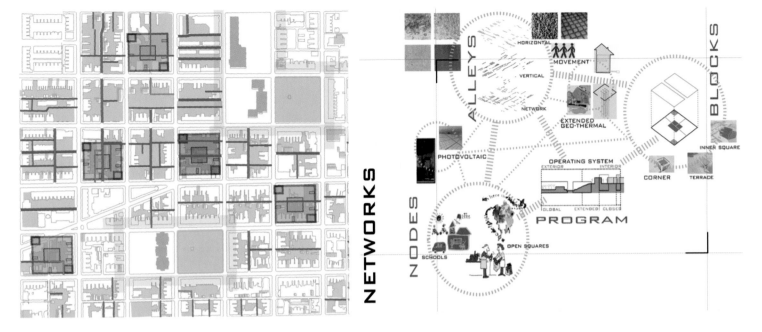

NETWORKS

ALLEYS

HORIZONTAL

MOVEMENT

VERTICAL

NETWORK

EXTENDED
GEO-THERMAL

PHOTOVOLTAIC

NODES

SCHOOLS

OPEN SQUARES

OPERATING SYSTEM

EXTERIOR   INTERIOR

GLOBAL   EXTENDED: CLOSED

PROGRAM

BLOCKS

INNER SQUARE

CORNER   TERRACE

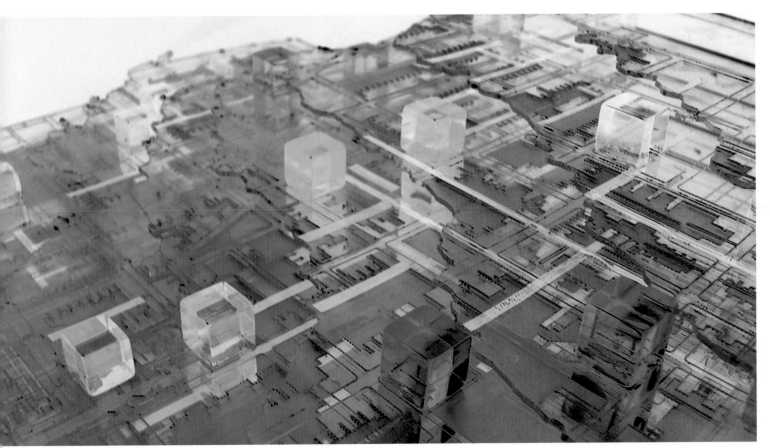

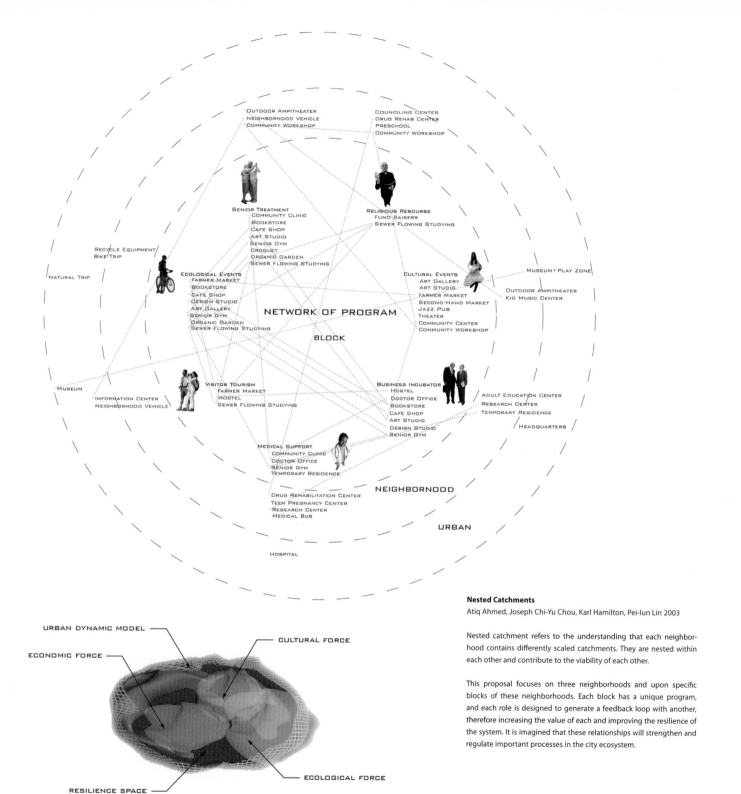

OUTDOOR AMPITHEATER
NEIGHBORHOOD VEHICLE
COMMUNITY WORKSHOP

COUNCILING CENTER
DRUG REHAB CENTER
PRESCHOOL
COMMUNITY WORKSHOP

SENIOR TREATMENT
COMMUNITY CLINIC
BOOKSTORE
CAFE SHOP
ART STUDIO
SENIOR GYM
CROQUET
ORGANIC GARDEN
SEWER FLOWING STUDYING

RELIGIOUS RESOURSE
FUND RAISERS
SEWER FLOWING STUDYING

RECYCLE EQUIPMENT
BIKE TRIP

NATURAL TRIP

ECOLOGICAL EVENTS
FARMER MARKET
BOOKSTORE
CAFE SHOP
DESIGN STUDIO
ART GALLERY
SENIOR GYM
ORGANIC GARDEN
SEWER FLOWING STUDYING

CULTURAL EVENTS
ART GALLERY
ART STUDIO
FARMER MARKET
SECOND-HAND MARKET
JAZZ PUB
THEATER
COMMUNITY CENTER
COMMUNITY WORKSHOP

MUSEUM+PLAY ZONE

OUTDOOR AMPITHEATER
KID MUSIC CENTER

NETWORK OF PROGRAM

BLOCK

MUSEUM

INFORMATION CENTER
NEIGHBORHOOD VEHICLE

VISITOR TOURISM
FARMER MARKET
HOSTEL
SEWER FLOWING STUDYING

BUSINESS INCUBATOR
HOSTEL
DOCTOR OFFICE
BOOKSTORE
CAFE SHOP
ART STUDIO
DESIGN STUDIO
SENIOR GYM

ADULT EDUCATION CENTER
RESEARCH CENTER
TEMPORARY RESIDENCE

HEADQUARTERS

MEDICAL SUPPORT
COMMUNITY CLINIC
DOCTOR OFFICE
SENIOR GYM
TEMPORARY RESIDENCE

NEIGHBORNOOD

DRUG REHABILITATION CENTER
TEEN PREGNANCY CENTER
RESEARCH CENTER
MEDICAL BUS

URBAN

HOSPITAL

Nested Catchments

Atiq Ahmed, Joseph Chi-Yu Chou, Karl Hamilton, Pei-lun Lin 2003

Nested catchment refers to the understanding that each neighborhood contains differently scaled catchments. They are nested within each other and contribute to the viability of each other.

This proposal focuses on three neighborhoods and upon specific blocks of these neighborhoods. Each block has a unique program, and each role is designed to generate a feedback loop with another, therefore increasing the value of each and improving the resilience of the system. It is imagined that these relationships will strengthen and regulate important processes in the city ecosystem.

URBAN DYNAMIC MODEL

CULTURAL FORCE

ECONOMIC FORCE

ECOLOGICAL FORCE

RESILIENCE SPACE

Site01_Harlem Park

Site02_Hollins Market

Site03_Washington Village

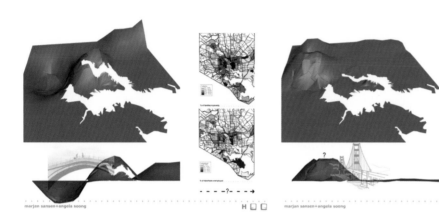

marjan sansen+angela soong

marjan sansen+angela soong

SAV - GOAL 1990

SAV - GOAL 2020

SAV - GOAL 2020 ??

CRAB PIER

BLUE CRAB

SAV - SUBMERGED AQUATIQ VEGETATION

CLEAN WATER

marjan sansen+angela soong

Liminal Landscape

Marjan Sansen and Angela Chen-Mai Soong, 2003

Crab farms and piers can contribute to the remediation of the bay. The Chesapeake blue crab needs SAV (submerged aquatic vegetation) in order for young crabs to survive. These SAV only grow in fairly clean water and in their turn, clean water. The crab, Baltimore's 'logo', becomes an indicator of an increasing water quality and social capital.

Besides the creation of job opportunities, a lacking element in the creation of an invisible bridge that crosses over social inequality is the informing of people. Firstly the neighborhood inhabitants, to detach the image of agriculture from slavery; secondly the not-neighborhood inhabitants, to SHOW people what is going on, so that a framework for social capital and eventually projects and small undertakings are created.

Seeing and smelling the polluted bay while visiting or buying crabs might inspire people to undertake something more than reading about it in one of many mailbox brochures, seeing and hearing vacant lots and drug traffic might in a similar way influence people's discussions or actions.

amelioration of the chesapeake bay water quality

nitrogen load · sediment load · industry reduced chemicals · crabs · 1982 · 1990 · 2000 · striped bass · acres of bay grasses · acres under nutrient management · miles restored forest

Infrared

Benjamin Batista-Roman, Matthew Priest, Marjan
Sansen, 2003

Baltimore seems to be characterized by social inequality
between the flourishing Inner Harbor and the emptying,
low-income downtown neighborhoods. The postindustrial economic shift currently replaces the landscape of
production with a landscape of decay. Reclaiming and
re-imagining underutilized places in the Watershed 263
area, we propose a linked system of Three Urban Filters
that respond to the city's complex needs.

1.US 40 'The Highway to Nowhere'
Phase One: Self – Generating Nature. The lowest part of
the highway to nowhere is subject to an approach of
laissez faire, to leave nature as it grows, creating a sunk-
en micro ecosystem, to be looked at but not to be accessed, like a world of nature's action.

Phase Two: Nature as process. Along the route of a now
extinct stream a storm water retention field functions
as a filter. In addition part of the US40 is proposed as a
soil remediation strip, receiving and treating the soil that
comes from the BandO site. This whole filtering process
serves as a trigger for further development; nursery, urban farming, and local markets.

Phase Three: Nature as a product – Regular well-main-
tained lawn texture sports fields and lawns are proposed
as recreation space for the neighboring schools and residents.

2. BandO Railroad
Reconfiguration of a geographic Barrier as a Multivalent
Threshold. Re-graded and reconceived as a linear park,
the BandO right of way provides storm-water retention/
filtration, and a bicycle and running path to the Gwynns
Falls Trail. In addition it provides north/south visual and
physical corridors between the upper neighborhoods
and Carrol Park.

3. Middle Branch
Inter-tidal warehouse emptying. Through a process of re-
generation of resources such as soils, and by reconfigur-
ing the usage of the surface area, the middle branch can
become the entry gateway to the city, an extension of
the sports arenas and a monitoring platform to the other
remediation processes proposed in this project.

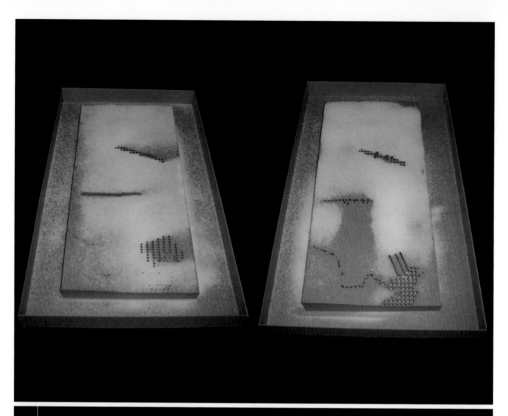

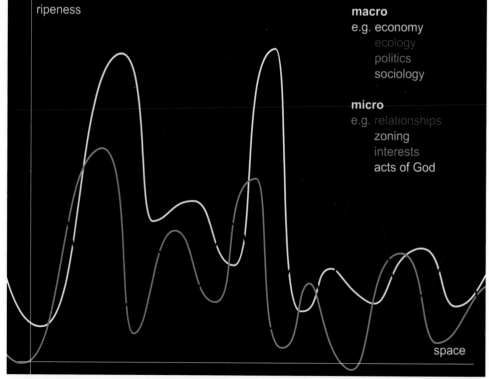

ripeness

macro
e.g. economy
ecology
politics
sociology

micro
e.g. relationships
zoning
interests
acts of God

space

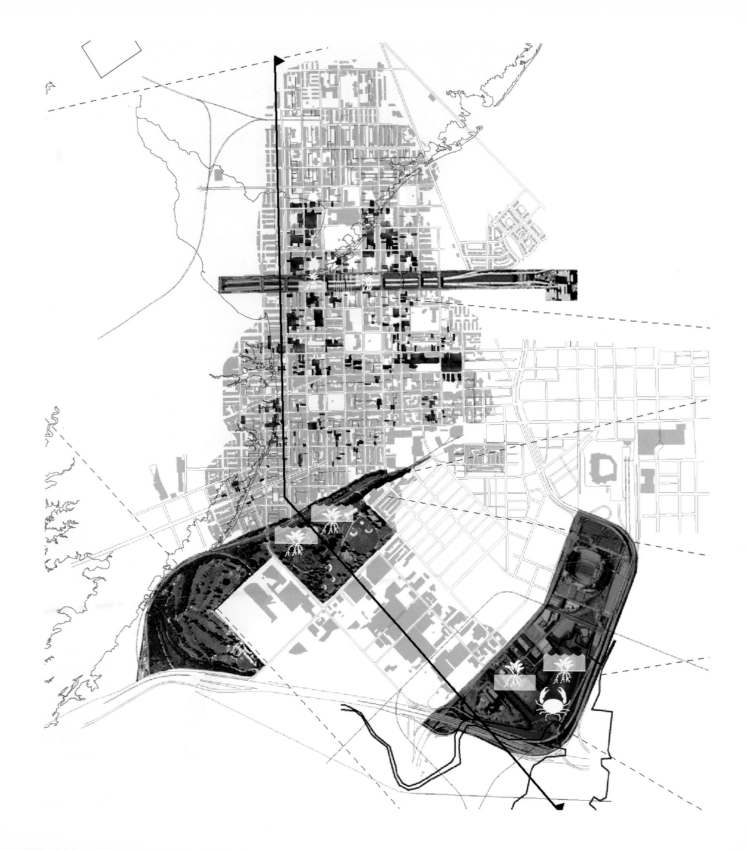

BOUNDARIES AS STRUCTURAL AND FUNCTIONAL ENTITIES IN LANDSCAPES: UNDERSTANDING FLOWS IN ECOLOGY AND URBAN DESIGN

DRS. M.L. CADENASSO AND S.T.A. PICKETT

Introduction: Structure and Function in Ecology and Design

The relationship between structure and function is fundamental to both ecology and design. In this brief introduction we outline key concepts for understanding boundaries in ecologically motivated design. The body of the chapter will expand and exemplify these concepts and relate them to urban designs. Ecologists and designers use some of the same terms to talk about the relationship between structure and function but the meanings often differ. As ecologists, we use these familiar terms in ecologically specific ways.

Practitioners in both disciplines must read the landscape in order to understand and work with it. A shared challenge is to observe the landscape at a space and time scale appropriate for the research or the design. Reading the landscape refers first to identifying the structural elements that make it up, the frequency with which they occur, and how they are arranged relative to each other. The structure of landscapes can be dissolved into patches. The constituent patches may contrast in their structure, composition, or process, as described in Chapter I. Descriptions of landscape structure can be pictorial, qualitative, or quantitative. Ecology seeks to describe and quantify landscape structure in an effort to understand how the system is organized. Ecology also explores what factors control and influence landscape structure, and how that structure changes through time. The second step in understanding a landscape requires knowing what certain elements do, how they interact, and how they influence each other—in other words, their function. Design practitioners read the landscape in an effort to create designs that work with the landscape rather than against it. Though the craft of design requires the isolation of a particular place in space and time, an awareness of the ongoing spatial and temporal context or setting of the design is necessary. Because the designed feature will not exist in isolation, how it interacts with adjacent features or will be influenced by past and ongoing dynamics of adjacent features should be considered in the initial design. A similar awareness of spatial and temporal context is needed in ecology.

Placing patches in their spatial context requires the recognition of boundaries between patches. This is true in both ecology and design. Boundaries both delimit patches and control the interaction between them. They may in fact be areas of heightened interaction in a designed or undesigned landscape. Boundaries also become a useful tool for manipulating the interactions within landscapes in ecology and design. The potential to act as hot spots of interaction gives boundaries their extraordinary significance.

The goal of this chapter is to use a single element of the landscape—boundaries—as a medium to expose parallels between ecology and design. Recognizing boundaries as structural and functional features of landscapes is a maturing area of research in ecology (Cadenasso and others 2003b). In this chapter we describe the concept of boundary and how it is defined structurally and functionally in ecology. We present a framework for boundaries that has emerged from ecology and suggest its application to design (Cadenasso and others 2003a). An analysis of how the boundary concept was used by students in the urban design and architecture studios at Columbia University demonstrates the utility of the boundary framework in synthesizing ideas from ecology and design.

Boundaries in Ecology

Landscapes divided into discrete elements consist of two kinds of structures: patches and boundaries. Though frequently depicted on maps as two dimensional, patches and boundaries are in fact three dimensional, extending above and below the surface. Contrasting patches in the landscape are determined based on some feature chosen as the characteristic of concern. For example, if the goal is to delineate betweening urban and rural areas, the landscape would be divided into patches that contrast in the kinds or densities of buildings, or in human population density, or some other index of urbanization (McIntyre and others 2000). If, however, the interest is in discriminating all sorts of land cover types, then the resulting patch array would look quite different (Figure 44). In addition to features that relate to urbanization, the more inclusive land cover classification might represent vegetation types, topography, soils and geology, hydrology, or various kinds of natural resource management and agriculture. These contrasting examples show that the same land area can be divided into multiple patch arrays depending on the contrast of interest. (See Chapter I for a more complete discussion of patches and patch dynamics.) Boundaries are structural and functional elements in the landscape that are located between contrasting patches. Though it is difficult to evaluate boundaries independently of patches, we will restrict this discussion to boundaries. We first discuss structural features of boundaries, and then move to their functional aspects.

Boundary structure

As structural elements, boundaries mark patch limits and are the zones of contact between two neighboring patches. Boundaries can be wide or narrow depending on how quickly the characteristic by which they are recognized changes. For example, the width of the boundary between two adjacent patches contrasting in plant structure would be determined by the spatial extent of the shift in plant structure. Forests adjacent to pastures differ in plant architecture where one consists of trees and the other of grass and herbaceous species. The transition from grass to tree architecture could be abrupt and the boundary narrow if maintenance by mowing prevented woody plant encroachment into the pasture. In contrast, a gradual boundary would exist in a situation without maintenance, where young and mature trees may become scattered in the pasture. Another pair of contrasts between sharp and diffuse boundaries also involves management versus an underlying environmental gradient. For example, patches of human settlement and remnant forests may have sharp boundaries between them, whereas the boundary between patch-

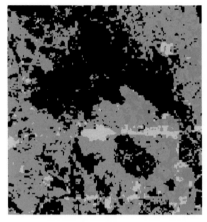
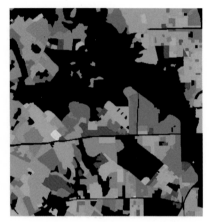

Figure 44. Two patch arrays for the same physical space. Each array uses different classification criteria to establish contrasting patches. In the left panel land cover is discriminated by low and high density residential, commercial/industrial, and forest land. A greater categorical resolution of land cover is shown in the right panel. Factors leading to contrasts in land cover include combinations of building types and density, vegetation texture and proportion, and the presence of impervious surfaces.

Boundary Framework

```
          Exchanges across boundaries
        ┌──────────────┼──────────────┐
Type of Exchange    Patch Contrast    Boundary Structure
 ├ Organisms         ├ Architecture     ├ Architectural
 ├ Matter            ├ Composition      ├ Compositional
 ├ Energy            └ Process          ├ Symbolic
 └ Information                          └ Perceptual
```

Figure 45. The boundary framework. The goal of the framework is to understand exchanges across boundaries. Boundaries may modulate those exchanges by inhibiting or facilitating their movement. How the boundary modulates exchanges will depend upon what is being exchanged, how the patches that the flow is moving between differ from one another, and features of the boundary itself. This framework is purposefully broad and it can apply to any system or spatial scale. The framework serves as a tool for generating models and hypotheses to test the role of boundaries in landscapes. The components of the framework must be specified for a particular field situation or model simulation (Modified from Cadenasso et al. 2003a).

es of marsh and meadow may be more gradual and subtle. The contrast in composition and structure between human settlement and forest is more distinct than the contrasts in composition and structure between a marsh and meadow established by subtle gradients of topography, soil and moisture.

Boundary function

The focus on boundaries as structural features can over-emphasize their static or descriptive aspect. Boundaries are also functional elements of the landscape and frequently their functional importance is disproportionate to the space they occupy. Patches in the landscape interact through the flows of organisms, material, and energy moving between them. Because boundaries exist between patches, they are necessarily traversed by and interact with the flows. Consequently, boundaries may control exchanges between patches in the landscape. Boundaries may prevent a flow from moving between two patches or they may facilitate that movement. How the boundary interacts with a specific flow depends on the identity of the flow and features of the boundary itself. These factors will determine the permeability of the boundary. For some flows, the boundary may be neutral, having no effect on its movement. A conceptual framework has been developed to identify and organize the major processes, system components, and types of system parameters required to understand boundary function. (Cadenasso and others 2003a, Figure 45). The framework is inclusive of systems and scales which must be specified when hypotheses and models are generated from the framework. The scope of this framework is encompassed in two central questions:

1. Do boundaries modulate flows between patches and, if so, what is the nature of the modulation, and what characteristics of the boundary contribute to that modulation?

2. If the boundary modulates flows between patches, does the modulation influence processes inside the interacting patches?

The framework aims to understand the phenomenon of exchanges across boundaries. Three components contribute to this phenomenon: 1) the type of exchange, 2) the nature of the contrast between patches, and 3) the structure of the boundary. Each of these components contains elements that must be specified for a particular field situation or model application.

Type of exchange can be materials, energy, organisms, or information. Exchange of materials may be exemplified by nitrogen carried in particles on the wind between field and forest. An example of the exchange of energy is the transfer of latent heat in water vapor moving between a coastal and inland patch. The daily movement of deer between forest shelter and food sources in open fields, and the transmission of a predator warning call from a bird perched on the forest edge are examples of the exchange of information across boundaries.

Contrasting patches can vary in architecture, composition, or process. An example of an architectural contrast is branching patterns of evergreen versus deciduous hardwoods. A compositional contrast is exemplified by a patch dominated by oaks versus one dominated by beech trees. A contrast in process is illustrated by a soil patch that converts nitrogen to its gaseous form versus a soil patch that converts it to the water soluble nitrate ion.

Features of the *boundary structure* that can influence the permeability of that boundary are architectural, compositional, symbolic, or perceptual. An example of an architectural feature affecting permeability is forest edge vegetation that alters the flux of water vapor and contributes to increased humidity in a forest interior. A shift in species composition from the host plant of a particular pest to an unfavorable species exemplifies a compositional influence on edge permeability for that pest. A habitat contrast that deters movement by forest interior birds, and patches of shrub clumps and open grassland that alter predation risk for small mammals illustrate symbolic or perceptual features that may influence cross patch exchanges.

In order to test the function of boundaries in regulating exchanges among patches, the elements that pertain to a particular situation need to be specified. There are no spatial or system constraints on this framework, and it can be applied to wild lands as smoothly as to urban centers. It can also be applied to systems of large size as well as to small areas. Obviously the exchange, patch contrast, and boundary structure would differ between urban and wild systems, but once the features of a system are specified, the framework can organize the approach used to understand the function of boundaries in both of these systems. In addition, by uniting the concept of boundaries in these two very disparate systems under the same framework, opportunities for synthesis and increased understanding can span differences in scale or disciplinary perspective.

The framework for ecological boundaries is a new contribution in ecology. The role that boundaries play in the landscape is an open question and is the topic of current debate and research within the science (Cadenasso and others 2003b). However, it is possible to summarize important structural and functional attributes of boundaries that have emerged from ecological studies (Cadenasso and others 2003a). We expect these points to be useful in translating the concept of boundaries from ecology to the practice of urban design:

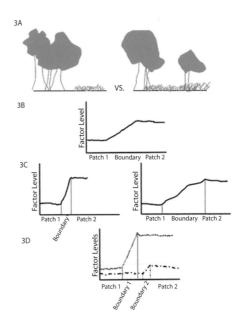

Figure 46. Abstractions of four of the boundary characteristics.

1. Boundaries may have some characteristics in common with the patches that they separate or they may be completely distinct. (Figure 46a)

2. Because the patches that the boundary separates are distinguished from each other by some defining characteristic, the gradient in that characteristic is steepest in the boundary compared to either of the neighboring patches. (Figure 46b)

3. Boundaries may be wide or narrow depending on the gradient of change between patches. (Figure 46c)

4. A boundary for one characteristic may differ in magnitude and location from a boundary defined by another characteristic. (Figure 46d)

5. The function of a boundary is determined by an organism, or by material, energy, information, or some process that is affected by the boundary gradient.

6. Boundaries are best construed as three dimensional volumes.

We will revisit these general characteristics to assess whether parallels can be drawn from the design realm.

Boundaries in Design

Boundaries in urban designs have structural and functional attributes, just as boundaries in ecological systems do. In the most simplistic form, boundaries delimit the area of the project and distinguish the area being designed from the area considered outside of the project. Boundaries are used in design as the places of contact between distinct parts of the design or between the design and its surroundings. In addition, boundaries identified as important in the urban system may be the focus of the design. Here we focus on the use of boundaries in these three ways as structural and functional elements of the design itself, not just as the design perimeter.

Boundaries can serve as indicators of different areas intended for different uses such as separating recreation, residential, and parking areas. Boundaries may exist as remnant structures, a past state of the system not removed during the creation of the new space, or be purposefully installed to create patches within the designed area. Boundaries may also perform aesthetic functions such as hiding garbage cans, utility meters, or the adjacent roadways.

Boundaries vary in their permeability and in the ways and extent to which they control exchanges among the parts of a design. The permeability can be influenced by the material selected for the construction of the boundary. For example, thorny shrubs will more effectively prevent children from crossing between a play area and a parking lot than low lying ground cover. A boundary constructed of wire fencing would perhaps be even less permeable. Material used to construct the boundary will depend on the exchange being controlled. Controlling the movement of people requires different materials than controlling the flow of water, for example. Boundaries can also be softened to invite people to cross them by decreasing slope or opening up vegetation.

There are many similarities in the concept of boundaries in ecology and design. Understanding of boundary structure and function in both disciplinary realms can be aided by the use of the conceptual framework presented earlier (Figure 45). Boundaries have structural features that can be directly manipulated by altering the composition, structure, or process forming them. The structure of the boundary influences its permeability, and boundary permeability varies for different exchanges traversing it. For example, thick trees between back yards and the adjacent roadway may be a barrier for elderly people unsteady on their feet but not for adventurous children. However, the same boundary may be a symbolic barrier when children are taught to respect the boundary and stay away from the road. The permeability or function of this boundary may change if its structure is altered by adding a paved pathway across it to facilitate the movement of people between the two adjacent patches of backyard and roadway.

An important question for urban design is how boundaries can be used to facilitate both socio-economic and ecological processes in urban systems. At the least, understanding the ecological and social effects of any boundaries introduced, or modified as a result of a design, may improve the ecological resilience of the design. What features of a design act as social, economic, or ecological boundaries? How are key ecological flows, such as of water, waste, pollution, exotic species, and resource subsidies for wild animals and pests governed by the boundaries the design includes? These are just some of the questions that designers might usefully ask about the impact of their designs on ecological boundary function. It is important to articulate the potential effects of the design on boundaries and their function. Having an appreciation of the ecological role of boundaries will increase the ability of designers to carry out the delicate hypotheses of optimization between the different functions their designs will influence.

The Principles of Boundaries in Design

We revisit the six principles of boundaries abstracted from ecology above (Figure.46a-d), to identify important ways to link the role of boundaries in design and ecology:

> 1. Boundaries may have some characteristics in common with the patches that they separate or they may be completely distinct. An example of common characteristics might be single family houses, where adjacent patches differ only in density of houses per unit area. In contrast, a distinct architectural boundary would be that between row houses and single family houses.

> 2. Since the patches that the boundary separates are distinguished from each other by some defining characteristic, the gra-

dient in that characteristic is steepest in the boundary compared to either of the neighboring patches. For example, solar exposure at street level would be expected to change most rapidly at the contact between zones of high rise versus low rise residential buildings. This change is, most likely, greater than the variation in solar exposure within each zone.

3. Boundaries may be wide or narrow depending on the gradient of change between patches. Investment in building maintenance may change gradually across space where rental versus owner-occupied units are interspersed, and sharply where zoning or habit of occupancy itself changes rapidly. These two gradients in ownership and zoning may not be located in exactly the same place.

4. A boundary for one characteristic may differ in magnitude and location from a boundary defined by another characteristic. Gradients of neighborhood greenness may reflect the spatial limits of community-oriented tree planting activity, while perception of crime risk may reflect gradients of police visibility.

5. The function of a boundary is determined by an organism, or by material, energy, information, or some process that is affected by the boundary gradient. Not all structural boundaries that are obvious in an urban system will have a function in terms of all kinds of flows. Material flows across some structural boundaries may be governed by infrastructure not by topography. "Storm sewer sheds" may link stormwater management across disparate architectural gradients. Information flows may be apparent to local residents and delimit neighborhoods, but be invisible to outsiders. Another way to state this principle is that deciding on a model of boundary structure and function depends on the choice of exchange(s) and patch contrasts.

6. Boundaries are best construed as three dimensional volumes.

The structural contrasts presented so cogently as maps and plans are actually perceived by people as volumes. The same is true of ecological flows—soil and atmosphere and infrastructure act as volumes within which contrast and gradients exist. Designers have a long tradition of expressing their projects in three dimensional models, or as oblique diagrams having perspective. Recognizing the additional parts of the volume that embody ecological processes will bring this principle to a higher level of utility.

How do such principles find expression in actual designs? We present examples in the next section, and analyze the way the projects express or assume boundary structure and function.

Merging ecology and design: examples from student works

The use of boundaries in design is well illustrated by the work of urban design students participating in studio courses at Columbia University. The studios focused on the Gwynns Falls watershed (GFW) in Baltimore, Maryland. This watershed is a focal research watershed of the Baltimore Ecosystem Study (BES) Long-Term Ecological Research Project (http:\\beslter.org). The 17,150 km^2 Gw-

Figure 47. "Stone filter." Rodrigo Guardia. The stone filter slows water moving downslope from the built neighborhood to the stream on the valley bottom. The filter slows water flow and captures particulates leading to a decrease in pollutants and a diminishing of erosion.

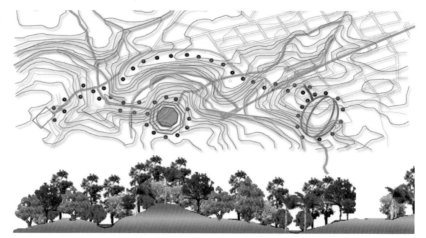

Figure 48. "Event space." Christiana Laryea. A design that alters the perceptual boundary between a neighborhood and adjacent greenway. This design shows an event space on the boundary which changes the perception from a barrier to a permeable boundary and, consequently, invites neighborhood residents into the greenway.

Figure 49. Terracing and revegetating the riparian zone within the 200 year flood plain (Pavithra Sriprakash). Reinforcing natural boundaries by strengthening the riparian upland boundary determined by gradients in topography and soil moisture. By terracing and revegetating this zone, the boundary between the built and adjacent stream system is made more discrete both structurally and functionally.

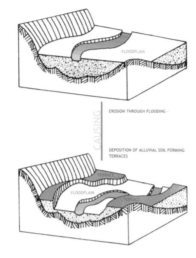

Figure 50. Exploding forests (Pavithra Sriprakash and Kratma Saimi). Extending the forest trees out into the adjacent neighborhood softens the built/non-built boundary. These fingers of trees serve as conduits into the adjacent greenway. Species can be unique to the fingers providing a source of identity to the neighborhoods.

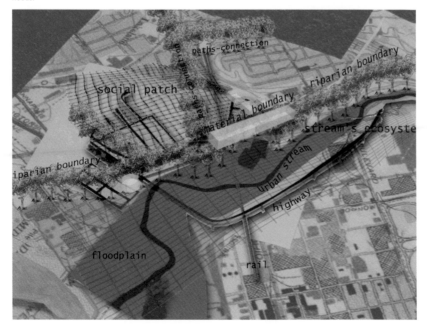

ynns Falls watershed extends from the Chesapeake Bay up through Baltimore City and into the surrounding Baltimore County. It is a dynamic area, with conversion of agricultural to residential and commercial land occurring in the headwaters, and residential and industrial abandonment in the lower reaches of the watershed. The BES uses a watershed approach to understand the urban system as an ecosystem. The watershed approach capitalizes on the stream as an integrator and relies on quantifying the influence of all types of processes in the watershed on water quality.

The Gwynns Falls watershed is physically, socially, and biologically heterogeneous. It can be divided into multiple patch arrays emphasizing different contrasts. For example, patches may be based on socio-economic status, density of vegetation or built structures, race, land use, topography, or zoning. In recent years, a consortium of non-profit groups and city agencies have created and implemented a plan for a trail and associated greenway to extend the length of the GFW from the headwaters down to the Chesapeake Bay. The greenway and adjacent built neighborhoods contrast sharply in structure and function. This heterogeneous and dynamic region was the subject of student design projects. Next, we discuss four projects that focused on the interaction of neighborhoods and adjacent portions of the greenway. We found these projects to implicitly or explicitly use a boundary concept that paralleled what we have articulated for ecology.

Project 1: Rodrigo Guardia

Gwynns Falls/Leakin Park is a large forested city park that contributes substantially to the greenway. The southern edge of the park is adjacent to the Rognel Heights neighborhood, a residential community consisting primarily of row houses. The park and the neighborhood are separated from each other by a two lane road. The topography of the park is steep, dropping down to the Gwynns Falls stream in the valley bottom. Rodrigo Guardia's design proposed a large stone filter to be installed at the outfall of a neighborhood storm drain at the edge of the park and running parallel to the hill's slope (Figure. 47). This filter would control the flow of water and associated particulates and pollutants between the built environment and the park. By slowing the flow of water runoff, the particulates of pollutants and soil could be captured, leading to a decrease in pollutant inputs and erosion.

Project 2: Christiana Laryea

The greenway is adjacent to many different neighborhoods as it traverses the GFW. These neighborhoods differ in the way in which the greenway is made visible to residents of the neighborhoods. For example, in some neighborhoods parking is available and prominent signs lead potential walkers to the trail. In other neighborhoods, less obvious signs announce its presence but, in some other cases, there are few or no signs (Figure 48). The interaction of people with the greenway may differ substantially among neighborhoods along its length because of differences in perception of the trail's safety and access. Christiana Laryea's project proposed to use the greenway as a conduit between neighborhoods by creating events and event spaces to draw residents into the greenway.

Projects 3 and 4: Kratma Saimi and Pavithra Sriprakash

These two projects were located near the base of the watershed and they focused on the interactions of people in the adjacent neighborhoods with the Gwynns Falls stream. One design proposed restoring the function of the floodplain by terracing and revegetating the streamside, or riparian, area within the 200 year flood zone (Figure 49). In both designs the boundary between the stream and the adjacent neighborhood was structurally distinct and walkways, abandoned roadways and rail lines were used to direct the flow of people between the two. The idea of an "exploding" forest was introduced as a way to connect the neighborhoods to the riparian zone (Figure 50). Forests of the riparian zone would be "exploded" by planting trees in continuous formation from the riparian zone out into the adjacent neighborhoods. Using different species of trees for each neighborhood would provide a source of identity for the neighborhoods.

Relating designs to the boundary framework

These four projects can each fit into the generalizable boundary framework that has emerged from ecology (Cadenasso and others 2003a). The goal of the framework is to understand how boundaries control exchanges among the patches of the landscape. The function of the boundary depends upon the nature of the contrasting patches, the identity of the exchange, and the structure of the boundary. Central to each of these projects are the contrasting patches of built and non-built environments. However, each differs in the exchange it is designed to control. The stone filter is concerned with the flow of water and associated soil particulates and pollutants, while the other projects focus on the flow of people. In each design, the structure of the boundary—its physical or perceptual structure—is designed to control the identified flow. The stone used in the filter is semi-permeable allowing water to pass but slowing its movement so that particulates can be trapped and damage to the hill slope through erosion can be diminished. By designing events and event space, the boundary between the greenway and neighborhoods is softened and residents are encouraged to cross it. This design does not alter the physical structure of the boundary, but rather adapts the perceptual structure to change it from a perceived barrier to a perceived permeable boundary. Finally, the planting of riparian vegetation and terracing of the floodplain creates or reinforces the boundary between the built and non-built environment. Using the 200 year flood level to make this boundary reinforces topographic and geologic gradients present in the system. The exploding forest design, in turn, softens the boundary at the upper end of the riparian zone by pulling the forest into the neighborhood. These fingers of forests can serve as trails leading people to the greenway and they can connect the neighborhood to the greenway symbolically as the fingers are perceived to be a continuation of the greenway.

Conclusions

In each design the three components of the boundary framework—patch contrast, type of exchange, and nature of the boundary—are identified. All of the designs intervene with the nature of the boundary to control exchanges. By adding the stone filter at the storm drain outfall, Guardia modifies the boundary between the neighborhood and the adjacent wooded slope. The filter changes the structure of the boundary and influences the timing and quality of the water being exchanged across that boundary. The water would be slowed down and particulates removed. By altering the boundary structure, the exchange of water across it is also modified and the result is potentially less erosion and pollution input for the wooded slope.

Projects by Laryea, Saimi, and Sriprakash all modify and revise the boundary to influence the exchange of people between neighborhoods and adjacent green spaces. They work with different features of the boundary to achieve this goal. Laryea alters the perception of the boundary from one of impermeability to permeability. This is done through a variety of mechanisms such as signs to increase awareness that the boundary is permeable, and events that adjust perceptions of the boundary and, consequently, the desire to cross it. Saimi and Sriprakash transform the structure of the boundary by planting trees. This filling in of the riparian zone not only returns ecological function to the zone but also allows the exchange of people between the neighborhood and the zone to be controlled. By using remnant walkways, rail lines, and abandoned roadways, they limit exchanges between the two patches of neighborhood and riparian zone to these conduits that cut through the boundary. Simultaneously, these designs use tree composition as a way to attract or draw people towards the boundary and encourage them to use the conduits to cross. This extends the "visibility" of the adjacent riparian zone into the neighborhoods.

Each of these designs reinforced, constructed, or made permeable the boundary between built and non-built patches. These projects demonstrate that the inclusive framework can be specified to a particular design. Though the projects differed in location and goals, they share a conceptual framework which facilitates their synthesis. The boundaries framework, in whichever disciplinary realm it is being used, retains the ultimate goal of understanding exchanges across boundaries. Such understanding can support the ability to make desirable and ecologically resilient urban designs.

Ecological definitions and examples of words used in this chapter:

Structural elements are features that give the landscape three dimensional form, such as trees, rocks, rivers, buildings, or highways.

Structure can refer to single elements such as a building or to an aggregation of elements such as a neighborhood. These two examples reflect different scales of structure.

Landscape is two or more patches that interact by exchanging organisms, material, or energy. Landscapes are scale neutral. They can be very small if considering exchanges between patches of shrubs and bare soil in the desert or very large if considering exchanges between continents and oceans, for example. The extent of the landscape is user defined.

Landscape structure defines patterns in the landscape that may be determined by contrasts in 1) the structure of the elements such as single story versus multistory buildings, 2) the type of elements, such as forests and fields, 3) how the elements are arranged in space relative to each other, or 4) processes. The contrasts in landscape structure are frequently depicted as patches (see Pickett and Cadenasso, this volume)

Boundary is a zone of transition delimiting two patches. Its three dimensional form extends from below the soil surface up into the atmosphere. Its width may vary depending on the criteria used to define the two adjacent patches. For example, a boundary between a forest and a field may be wide for changes in air temperature but narrow for changes in species composition.

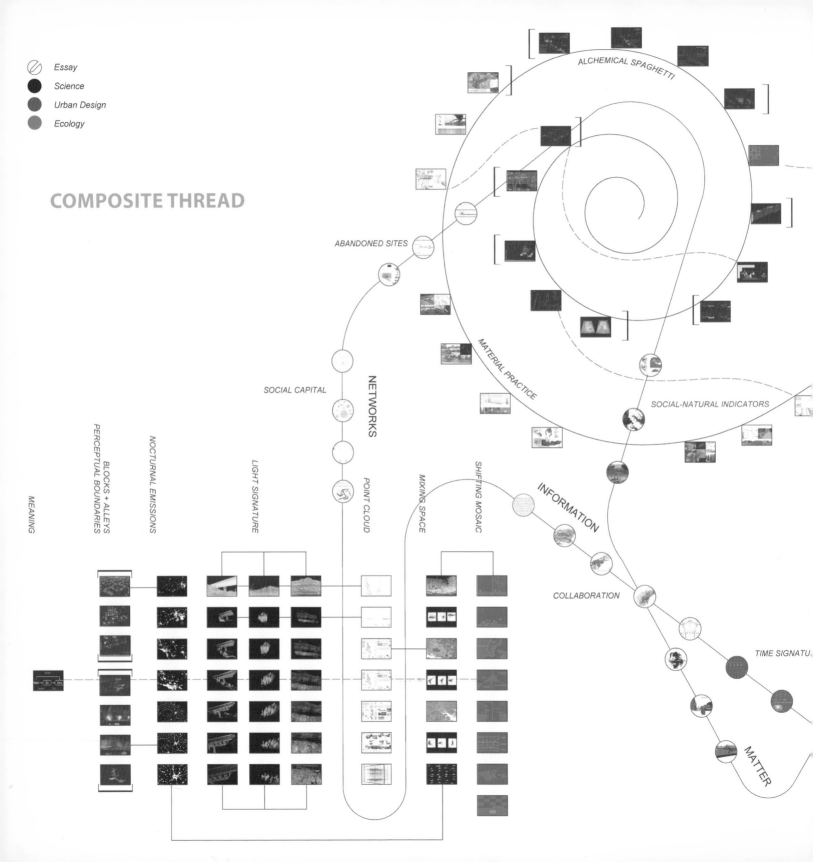

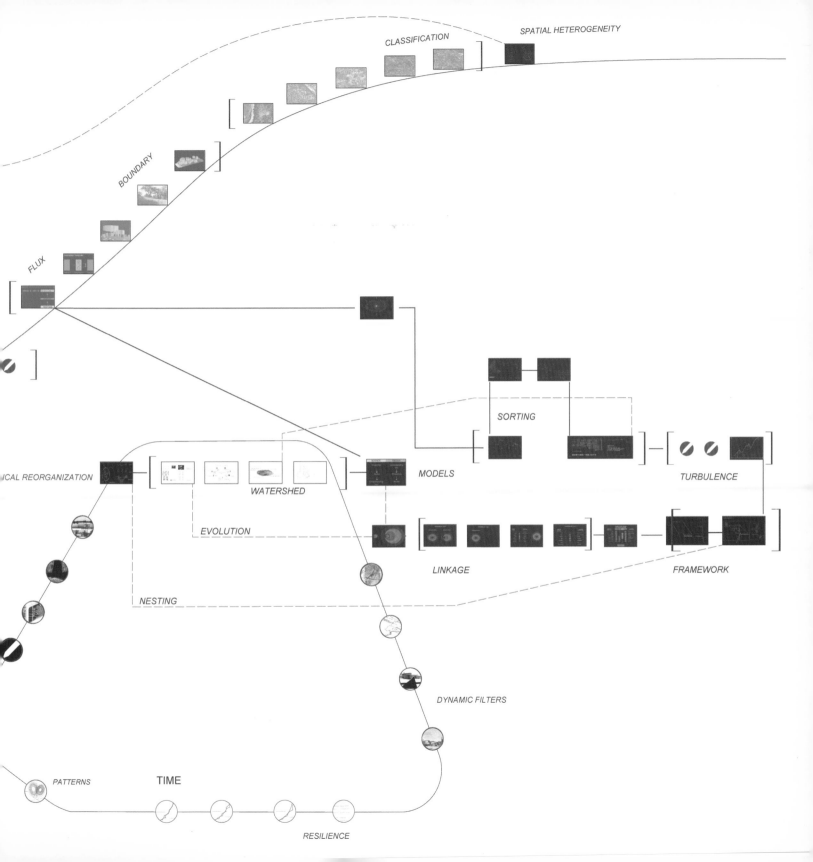

SPATIAL HETEROGENEITY

CLASSIFICATION

BOUNDARY

FLUX

SORTING

MODELS

TURBULENCE

ICAL REORGANIZATION

WATERSHED

EVOLUTION

LINKAGE

FRAMEWORK

NESTING

DYNAMIC FILTERS

PATTERNS

TIME

RESILIENCE

modeling social capital: ideological linking

- Social capital is dependent upon conditions of social interaction (e.g. bond, bridge, link).
- Social interaction is based on the ideological relationships among actors within a given territory, a "neighborhood."
- These relationships can be understood in terms of the "strength" and "direction" of the link (social interaction) that determine the flow of ideas, resources, and support that constitute social capital.

Modelling Social Capital: Ideological Linking
Justin Moore, Manolo Figueroa, Angela Chen-Mai Soong,
Flora Hsiang-I Chen 2003

Rather than taking neighborhood boundaries as the location of difference, this project uses a network model to construct the social capital of Watershed 263.

Social capital is dependent upon conditions of social interaction (e.g. bond, bridge, link). Social interaction is based on the ideological relationships among actors within a given territory, a 'neighborhood.' These relationships can be understood in terms of the strength and direction of the link (social interaction) that determine the flow of ideas, resources, and support that constitutes social capital.

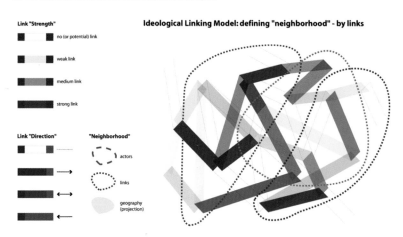

Link "Strength"
- no (or potential) link
- weak link
- medium link
- strong link

Link "Direction"

"Neighborhood"
- actors
- links
- geography (projection)

Ideological Linking Model: defining "neighborhood" - by links

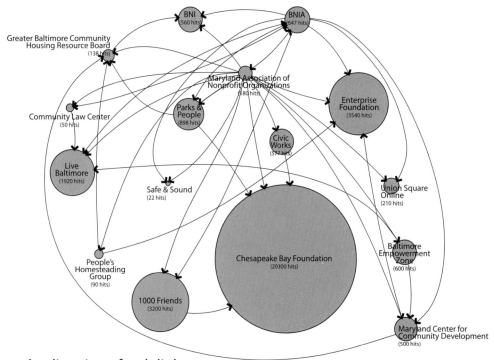

direction of web link

area determined by weight of web presence - i.e. # of hits @ www.google.com

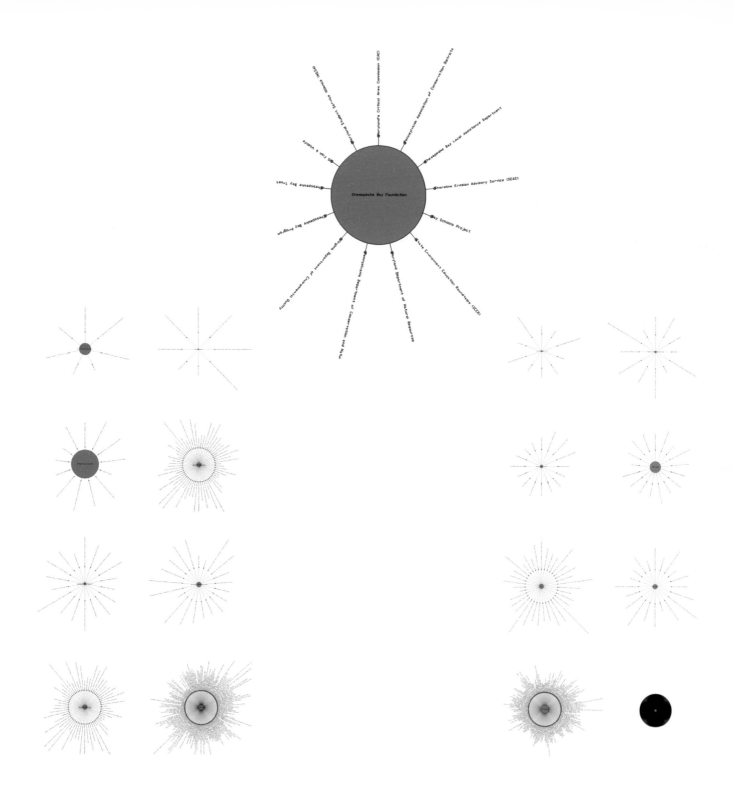

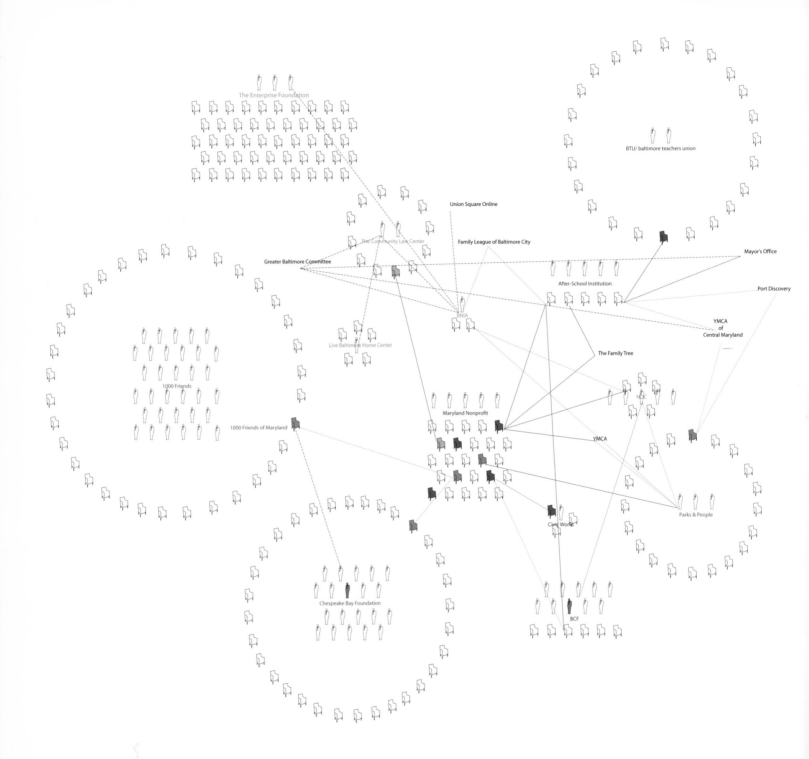

The Enterprise Foundation

BTU/ baltimore teachers union

Union Square Online

The Community Law Center

Family League of Baltimore City

Greater Baltimore Committee

Mayor's Office

After-School Institution

Port Discovery

BNIA

Live Baltimore Home Center

YMCA
of
Central Maryland

The Family Tree

1000 Friends

NDC

Maryland Nonprofit

YMCA

1000 Friends of Maryland

Parks & People

Civic Works

Chespeake Bay Foundation

BCF

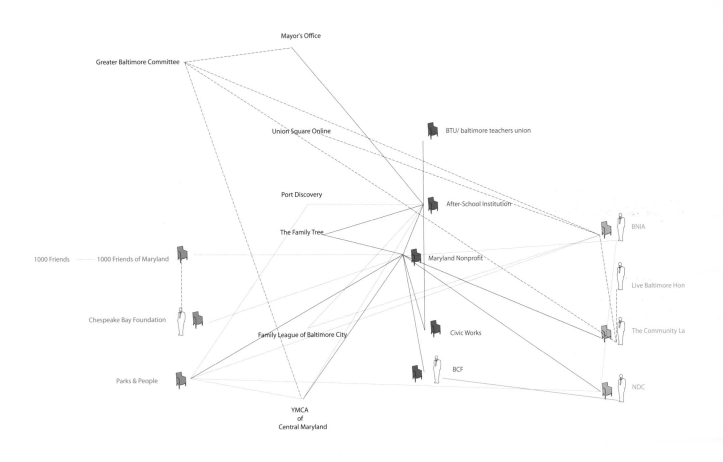

Mayor's Office

Greater Baltimore Committee

Union Square Online

BTU/ baltimore teachers union

Port Discovery

After-School Institution

The Family Tree

BNIA

1000 Friends   1000 Friends of Maryland

Maryland Nonprofit

Live Baltimore Hon

Chespeake Bay Foundation

The Community La

Family League of Baltimore City

Civic Works

Parks & People

BCF

NDC

YMCA
of
Central Maryland

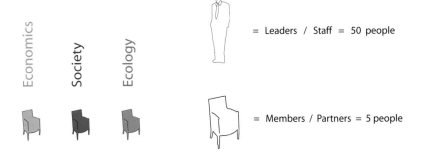

Economics

Society

Ecology

= Leaders / Staff = 50 people

= Members / Partners = 5 people

Point Cloud: Watershed Catchment Study II
Flora Hsiang-I Cheng, Manolo Figueroa, Justin G. Moore,
Camellia Han Tian, Oliver Valle, 2004

Point Cloud: Watershed Catchment Study
Flora Hsiang-I Cheng, Manolo Figueroa, Justin G. Moore,
Camellia Han Tian, Oliver Valle, 2003

This project uses a point cloud signature. Rather than
being just an analytical tool it is an urban design model
for Watershed 263.

Taking the 'image' of the point cloud as a powerful metaphor, this project is successful as it works on multiple
levels, in particular, those of perception and scale.

Our project fuses several distribution patches at work
in Watershed 263; surface and storm water, grey and
wastewater, debris, vegetation, and property (value).
These patches are understood as 'point clouds' that can
be interpolated to define strategies and interventions
across the entire watershed. Together these serve to re-
imagine the operative and experienced 'nature' of Baltimore's Inner city.

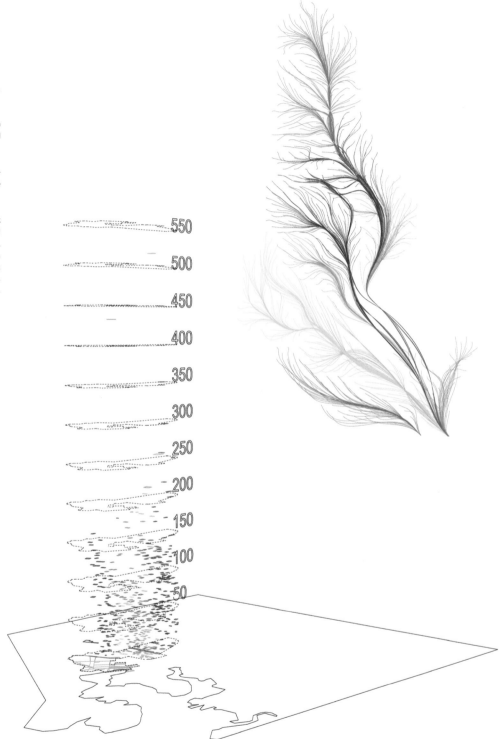

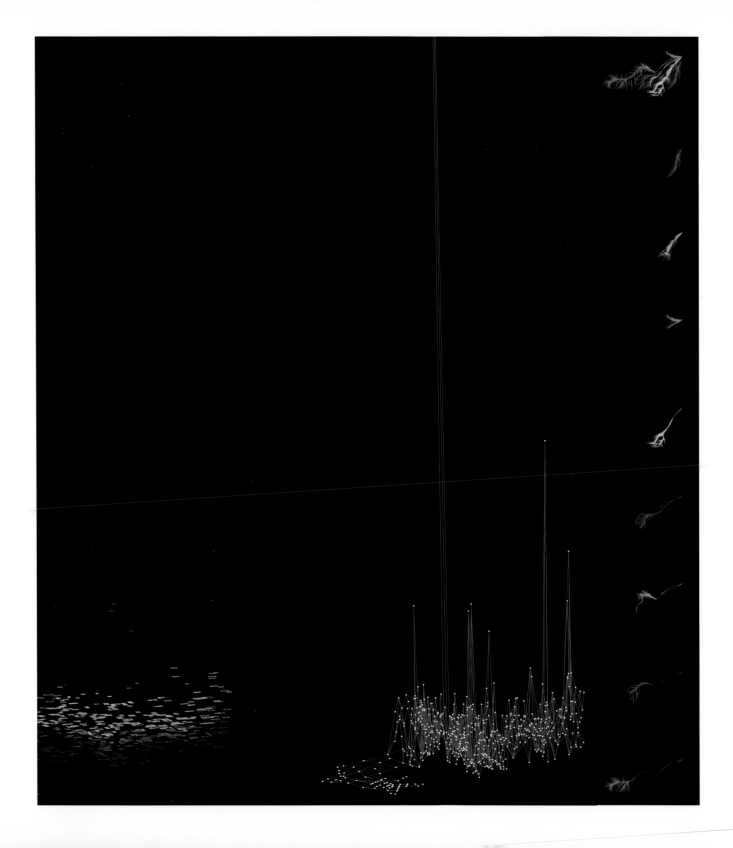

**Point Cloud Emergence
(this page)**

The site and issues defined by Watershed 263 in Baltimore's inner city encompass a range of ecological, economical, and social conditions and problems, from the polution of the Chesapeake Bay, to the devaluation of property, to limited community stewardship and involvement. The frame established by the problematic of the watershed provides an opportunity for the urban design project to consider these multiple issues collaboratively and break out of the established territories for action.

point_cloud

COMPOSITE POINT CLOUD

550
500
450
400

**Point Cloud Emergence
(opposite page)**

This point cloud framework requires that the urban design strategies/ interventions operate foremost at the local scale. The larger site can be understood via various patches that begin to formulate criteria for design interventions. The project then creates a strategy that is exercised at the level of the block based on a new surface paradigm for the urban site that is informed by the interlaced point clouds at any given location. This paradigm serves to dissolve once contained or segregated urban systems into a shared field of points, flows, and territories that play out dynamically over time.

emergence

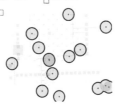

patch interlace

dynamic flow analysis

property control
redistribution

planting patches

block mosaic

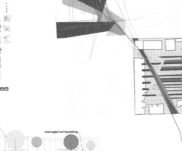

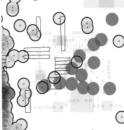

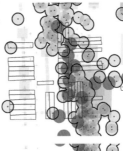

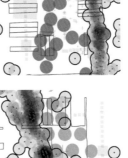

share+hold

re(circulate)

aqualung

containerscape

changing garden

grey water storage

storage/composting

vending/shelter

share+hold   aqualung   containerscape

section through block mosaic

Point Cloud: Board II
Flora Hsiang-I Cheng, Manolo Figueroa, Justin G.
Moore, Camellia Han Tian, Oliver Valle, 2004

red
blue

projection

mound
container

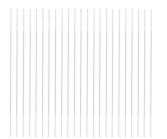
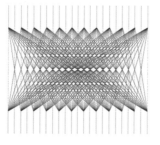
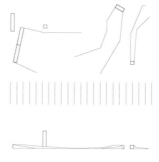

block strategy

permeable surface
impermeable surface (trash)
impermeable surface (water)

permeable surface
impermeable surface (trash)
impermeable surface (water)
tree/ canopy

permeable surface
impermeable surface (trash)
impermeable surface (water)
tree/ canopy
fence

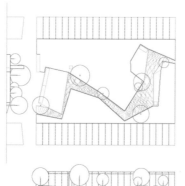
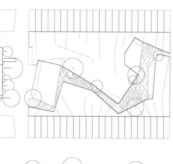

vacant lots

puddle prevention area

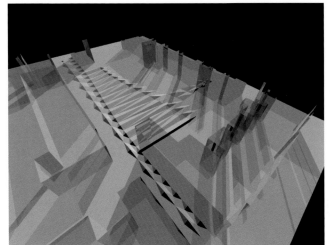

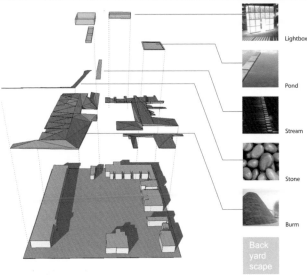

Lightbox

Pond

Stream

Stone

Burm

Back yard scape

| A
P
R | M
A
Y | J
U
N | J
U
L | A
U
G | S
E
P | O
C
T | N
O
V | D
E
C |

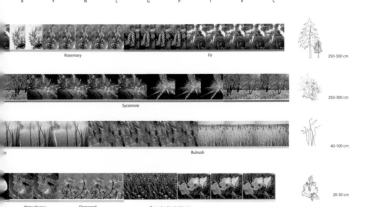

Rosemary   Fir   250-300 cm

Sycamore   250-300 cm

Bulrush   40-100 cm

Water Poppy   Dogwood   Zantedeschia Aethiopica   20-30 cm

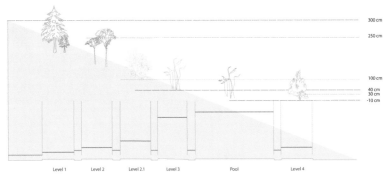

300 cm

250 cm

100 cm

40 cm
30 cm
-10 cm

Level 1   Level 2   Level 2.1   Level 3   Pool   Level 4

Point Cloud: Board III
Flora Hsiang-I Cheng, Manolo Figueroa, Justin G.
Moore, Camellia Han Tian, Oliver Valle, 2004

Wetland Bridge crossing over the I-40

Inner Block Wet Programming

Controlled Ponding_ Diggs Joh

Cross Subjectivation

Habitat Replication

Flower Garden for the Obsessive/Compulsive

Playground Flooding_ Frederick Elementary

ddle School

Landscapes of Uncertainty and Mystification_ Proposed North Access to Frederick Elementary

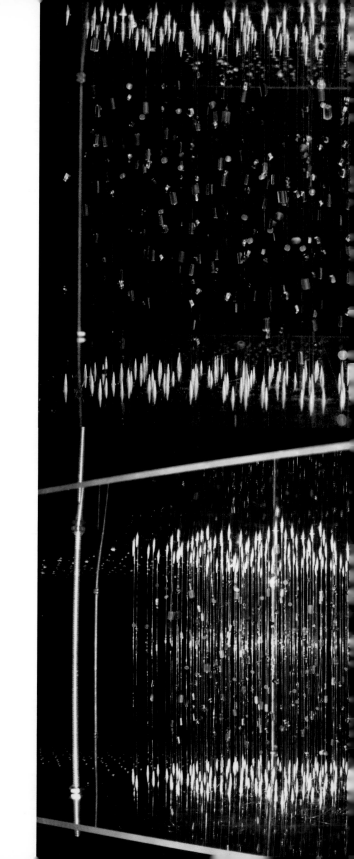

Point Cloud: Model Photo

Flora Hsiang-I Cheng, Manolo Figueroa, Justin G. Moore, Camellia Han Tian, Oliver Valle, 2004

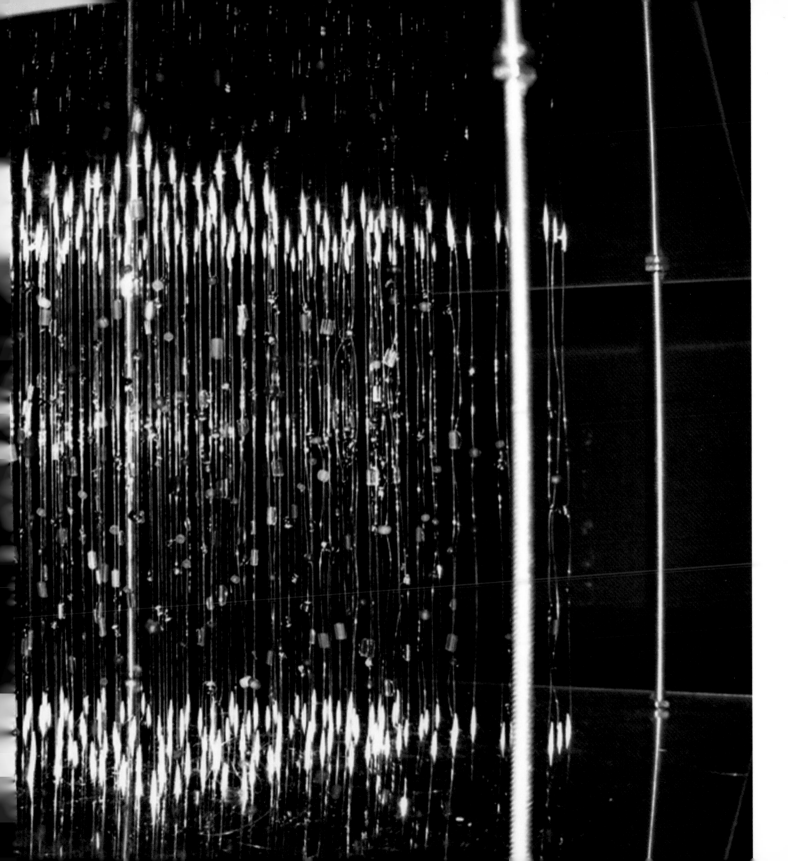

URBAN DESIGNS AS MODELS OF PATCH DYNAMICS

BRIAN MCGRATH

Drs. Steward Pickett and Mary Cadenasso close Chapter II with this deceptively straightforward challenge: in order to link ecology and design, start by making urban designs themselves working models of ecosystems. This chapter argues that Pickett and Cadenasso's vision questions prevailing limits of both avant-garde and sustainable approaches to architecture and suggests the creation of a new field between ecology and architecture.

Nature and cities can no longer be seen as distinct systems. The mutual interrelations and feed-back loops among biophysical, socio-ecological, and built environment practices must be the foundation of urban patch dynamics. Avant-garde architecture has successfully grabbed public attention and engaged the individual human psyche, while sustainable design is laudable for its environmental and social accomplishments. However, the discrete methods from architecture and ecology remain inadequate in analytically describing or achieving sensibility within the vast interconnected ecosystems of the contemporary city. Designed urban patches combine these two approaches to link human behavior and cultural meaning within larger ecosystem patterns and processes. The heterogeneity, modularity, flexibility, and resilience of designed urban dynamics improve our ability to positively influence our increasingly complex world. With this new paradigm, cultural circuits of architectural perception can be adapted toward inhabiting urban ecosystems in creative and inclusive ways. Cities, using patch dynamics as a catalyst, become understandable as intelligent patterns of change and flows at an array of interrelated scales.

Patch dynamic theory fundamentally alters ecological and architectural thinking and challenges the way nature and cities are conventionally understood. According to Pickett and Cadenasso, the fundamental ecological paradigm has shifted away from the narrow and exclusive ecology of the equilibrium model to the broad and inclusive ecology of non-equilibrium. Previous assumptions that ecological systems are closed, highly deterministic, bounded, and internally regulated have been replaced by the opposite: systems are now seen to be open, often regulated from the outside, and probabilistic (Pickett and Cadenasso 2002).

Pickett and Cadenasso urge architects to explicitly incorporate the patch dynamic framework as both a constraint and a driver of urban design, making designs themselves experimental models "…as vehicles to test the assumptions and processes of patch dynamics in the arena of built spaces." Urban design modeling is therefore conceived as a collaborative activity in this new field between architecture and ecology, taking place through computer simulations, testing and monitoring of urban ecosystems, and experimental participatory design proposals in diverse social contexts.

Creating urban designs that are contemporary cultural models of patch dynamics first requires expanding our understanding of the word model, leading to urban design practices where conceptualization, experimentation, and design are collapsed as one coordinated activity. Here, we will consider urban design modeling as a transversal activity between ecology and architecture, pointing to a trans-disciplinary meta-methodology (Genosko 2002) in which urban design models negotiate among different disciplines, actors and methods as well as the dynamics of constituencies, programs, and scales.

This chapter creates a design framework for urban patch dynamics by correlating the specificity of Robin Evan's three geometries of architecture - compositional, projective and signified (1995) - with Felix Guattari's three ecologies - the psyche, socius and environment (2000). Such a framework makes evident to mobile, sensate human observers the four dimensions of urban ecosystem processes within a range of scales and sites. Ecological, social and ethical design processes can be made sensible by engaging daily life in dynamic feed back processes. Urban designers will play essential cultural roles by translating scientific theories and models into the physical experience within the spatial practices of everyday life, resulting in an inhabited model of urban patch dynamics.

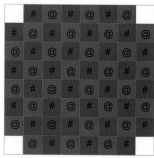

An Integrated City. Even if people insist that a minimum fraction of their neighbors resembles themselves, it is possible to create an equilibrium residential pattern that is highly integrated.

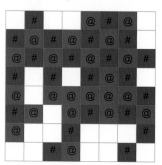

Perturbing the Equilbrium. If the pattern is given some random scrambling, some individuals are no longer content with their location.

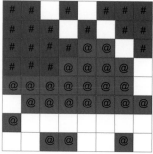

A Segregated City. The result is a chain reaction in which each move provokes other moves; in the end, mild concerns about being in a local minority produce a completely segregated city.

Modeling Discourse

In *Good City Form*, Kevin Lynch calls attention to the difference between the use of the word "model" in science and design. For scientists, a model is a speculative description of a system's structure and function, while for designers a model is a normative idea or mental image of an object or form which can be imitated. Lynch ignores the scientific meaning of model in order to secure a working definition for urban design. "A model is a mental picture of how the city ought to be made; a succinct description of urban form or process which is a prototype to follow." For Lynch, urban design decisions are largely based on prescriptive mental pictures already in the head of the designer. However, an integrated city theory - a succinct explanation of the inner workings of a formerly confusing phenomenon - will produce new urban models, whose visualization creates a mental structure of a collective philosophical and psychological construction shared by city inhabitants (1981).

Lynch's classic example of a normative urban design model is the Baroque City's axial network: symbolic landmarks are located at commanding points in the terrain, connected by major streets with controlled, unified façades. It is both an aesthetic model and a strategy for the application and stabilization of centralized power (Lynch 1981). In Pickett's ecological terms, the Baroque City is an older equilibrium model, executing power by employing strong visual effects, public symbolism, and a memorable general structure to achieve sensibility. Public resources are deployed to maintain political and social stability via a highly ordered and hierarchical urban design. However, Anita Berrizbeitia, points out that the Grand Canal at Vaux-le-Vicomte is in fact the River Monceaux, rerouted through the garden. The axial order of both the chateaux and the canal masks the subtle dynamics of river and garden, diverting the stability of the formal abstract order (2002). In looking for the memorable and easily imaginable formal models, has Lynch dispensed with the ability of urban design models to speculate on the dynamic and the complex?

Contemporary urban design must broaden Lynch's definition of "model." Expanding the term takes account of structural and functional models from urban ecology and economics, while critically reassessing Lynch's theories on city image, form and process. Patch dynamic models do not assume equilibrium, but measure and predict changes in disturbance, succession, and ecosystem both spatially and temporally. Urban designs as models of patch dynamics redirect the focus of contemporary architecture in order to embody complex processes whose patterns of change are experienced by our sensate bodies. The resulting experiential knowledge encourages new psychological, social and environmental relations.

Modeling Urban Ecosystem Complexity

In response to the daunting challenges of global urbanization, Manuel Castells has called for an urban design perspective to connect an eco-social approach with a techno-economic study in the context of a comparative cultural framework (2001). This section examines how the cultural framework of an urban design perspective can connect the techno-economic complexity of cities, as defined by Paul Krugman's economic self-organization models),with Simon Levin's eco-social models of nature. Krugman's models explain urbanization processes while accounting for patterns within emerging urban systems. Levin's models of complex adaptive ecosystems reveal how local interactions create diversity and resilience in nature (Krugman 1996; Levin 1999). As cities are formed by both ecological and economic processes, urban designs as models of patch dynamics engage economic self-organization and ecosystem resilience as a basis for the understanding of socio-natural urban complexity.

For Krugman, urban development follows principles of spatial self-organization in which order arises through the tension created between short range centripetal and long range centrifugal economic forces. Self-organizing systems emerge from almost homogeneous or random states to create large-scale clustered patterns, which are a result of unstable

Figure 51 (opposite). Schelling's Segregation Model. Self organization does not always produce desirable results (Redrawn from Krugman, Paul. 1996.The Self Organizing Economy. Malden, MA: Blackwell Publishers.)

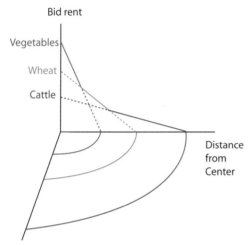

Figure 52. The Von Thunen-Mills Model. Land around a town organizes into concentric rings of production (Redrawn from Krugman, Paul. 1996. The Self Organizing Economy. Malden, MA: Blackwell Publishers.)

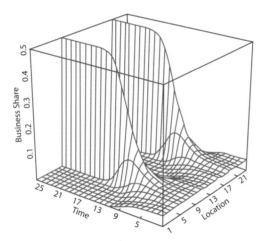

Figure 53. The Evolution of Edge Cities. An initially almost uniform distribution of businesses across the landscape evolves spontaneously into a highly structured metropolis with two concentrated business districts (Redrawn from Krugman, Paul. 1996. The Self Organizing Economy. Malden, MA: Blackwell Publishers.)

fluctuations, random growth, and frequency distributions. The spatial models described by Krugman range in scale from the social interactions of households within neighborhoods to regional business location decisions. Schelling's Segregation Model (Figure51) reveals that integrated residential patterns tend to be unstable as decisions to move result from highly localized perceptions. The Von Thunen-Mills Model (Figure 52) describes how competition for land around a town leads to the emergence of concentric rings of production. Central Place Theory demonstrates the dispersal of cities within a hierarchical constellation of nested catchments (Page 48, Figure20). Lastly, the Edge City Model (Figure 53) explains the emergence of a polycentric pattern of businesses into multiple yet clearly separated commercial centers strung along peripheral highways, with dispersed residential areas radiating from these centers (Krugman 1996).

Economic cycles of adjustments and change are ruled by temporal self-organization. A complex dynamic economy will exhibit a pattern that in evolutionary theory is known as punctuated equilibrium: long periods of relative quiet, divided by short periods of rapid change (Figure 54). Herbert Simon's Urban Growth Model consists of "lumps and clumps". These new units of economic activity almost always form in existing clusters, creating a stratified and diverse urban center as well as new rings of growth. The study of Complex Landscapes depicts how the dynamic economic systems of business cycles shape over time. In percolation economics, temporal order arises from instability based on critical levels of inventory. Nonlinear Business Cycle Theory argues that steady growth is unstable; instead, pulses of expansion and contraction occur around long-run trends (Krugman 1996). Urban design in practice has been long subject to the boom and bust of real estate cycles rather than engaging time as a productive material.

Biologist Simon Levin argues that "…the biosphere is a Complex Adaptive System in which the never-ending generation of local variation creates an environment of continual exploration, selection, and replacement." Ecosystem adaptation is an unfolding game of chance with "instructions" not specified. Simple rules govern change. Natural selection tinkers, working

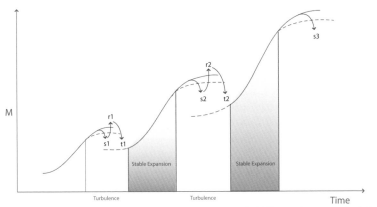

Figure 54. Punctuated Equilibrium. Economies tend to have periods of expansion before reaching a point of turbulence (Redrawn from Arrighi, Giovanni. 1994. The Long Twentieth Century, London: Verso.)

Building Resilience
Simon Levin's Fragile Dominion

1. Reduce Uncertainty
   - monitor
   - spread risks
   - form groups
2. Expect Surprise
   - adaptively manage and probe
   - build flexible response systems
3. Maintain Heterogeneity
4. Sustain Modularity
5. Preserve Redundancy
6. Tighten Feedback Loops

Table 2. Complex Adaptive Systems. Seeing the city as a complex adaptive system means we must translate the mechanisms of biology to urban design.

as a local mechanism relying on a constant generation of slight modification of existing patterns and choosing among them based on what works best. For Levin, the integrated evolution of a whole system is explained as "… an interplay among changes at a spectrum of scales." Levin explains that the evolutionary tendency for an ecosystem is to reach the edge of criticality at which extinction and speciation are constantly occurring, maintaining the variation needed for adaptability. In both biology and economics, equilibrium is a special case in a landscape of criticality, diversity, and uncertainty at the local level. Levin's ecosystem models demonstrate how species variety and heterogeneity depend on co-evolutionary processes; selection acts at small scales where feedback loops - incentives - are tight. However, there is no guarantee that local change is good for the system as a whole, because global feedbacks are weak and act over long time scales in ecology as well as in society (Levin 1999). Likewise, Krugman views socio-economic self organization as something we observe and try to understand, not necessarily something we want. For example, segregation and edge city sprawl are self-reinforcing processes but not necessarily good things.

Feedback influences the environment at multiple scales. Tight feedback loops and local decisions multiply to form large scale patterns. For instance, Levin shows how macroscopic patterns of biota mediate climate. The inventive ecosystem models Levin describes look beyond single organisms to seek knowledge about species mutualisms, ecological communities, reciprocal altruism, enlightened self-interest, and exploitative relationships.

Steven Johnson (2002) defines morphogenesis as an emergent process in which organisms assemble themselves without a master planner calling the shots. Simple agents following simple rules can create amazing complexity. Urban morphogenesis represents emergent, bottom-up behavior which decentralizes thinking and organizes space from below. Complex behaviors of urban systems consist of multiple agents interacting in varied ways, following local rules and oblivious to any higher-level instructions. Johnson identifies four key principals for complex behavior in cities, all of which could be employed in urban design: neighborhood interaction, pattern recognition, feedback, and indirect control. Similarly, Levin identifies six methods for maintaining a resilient complex adaptive system: reduce uncertainty, expect surprise, maintain heterogeneity, preserve redundancy, and tighten feedback loops (Table 2).

Spatial and temporal self-organization processes are evident in any city. The contemporary city is marked by both hyper- and post-urbanization as some uses cluster together creating dense agglomerations, while others disperse in an exurban sprawl. Growth occurs in spatially differentiated punctuated rhythms, resulting in urban development phase space. Physical traces are left from multiple economic cycles with specific ways of constructing landscapes. Increasingly unstable and uneven development creates patches of dense and loose urban types which constitute the ecologically and economically differentiated 21st century city: soft and hard, porous and impermeable, rich and poor. As rings of different building and urban types overlap and disperse over time, cycles of obsolescence, abandonment and reuse produce spatial heterogeneity and economic resilience in the system as a whole, but often generate neglected local pockets of poverty that are out of phase with ecological and social recovery cycles.

The spatial and temporal disturbance and succession of the patch dynamic ecological model cannot be represented in two-dimensional maps. Each distinct heterogeneous patch has three-dimensional boundaries to control flows of materials, energy, organisms, and information from patch to patch, which change over time (Pickett and Cadenasso 2002). The four dimensions which account for spatial configuration and time constitute the essence of urban patch dynamics. Urban patches present an explicit way to inhabit the world, and alert us to dynamic processes within that world.

Urban designs as models of patch dynamics, while benefiting from global thinking, are first enacted locally. Bottom-up decision making integrates economic and ecological models of complex adaptive and emergent systems using local designs as nodes in feedback loops. Feedback can influence the total environment at multiple scales. The subtle interplay between ecological and evolutionary events represents the integration of processes along a continuum of scales rather than a dialogue between two sharply distinguished ones. Watersheds, from small sub-catchments to regional river and estuary systems, serve as a precise scaling device. Feedback emerges within multiple time scales - from daily life to long term intergenerational cycles. Urban ecosystem logic is situated within the rings of phase space at the intersection of economic, ecological, and human patch dynamics. An urban design perspective located within that four-dimensional space is a powerful tool empowering agents rather than depending on a normative urban design model's systems of control and regulation.

A Framework of Three Ecologies and Three Geometries

Felix Guattari (2000) apprehends the world through three ecologies: the nascent individual *psyche*, a constantly mutating "*socius*" (social locus), and an *environment* in the process of being reinvented. He calls for eco-aesthetic inspiration to reverse the deterioration of individual and collective human life and the degradation of experience due to the intense

3 GEOMETRIES

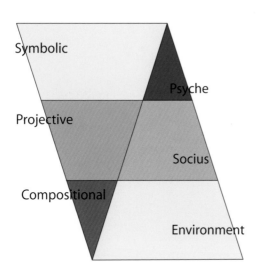

Figure 55. Urban Design Framework. Design is composition, projection and creating meaning in the three ecologies of the psyche, the socius and the environment.

3 ECOLOGIES

technological transformation of the earth. It is not only species that are becoming instinct, but also "… the words, phrases, and gestures of human solidarity." For Guattari, ecologies of the imagination will reinvent the relations of subjects to their bodies and the passage of time, as antidotes to mass-media manipulation, telematic standardization, and the conformism of fashion. Social ecology consists in developing specific practices that will modify and reinvent the ways in which we live together. The former griddings of society are replaced by "spontaneous existential territories." For Guattari, the ways of living on this planet are in question, and he calls for a revolution of the domains of sensibility, intelligence and desire in every day life (Figure 55).

Robin Evans theorizes architecture not as an autonomous discipline, but as a highly specific practice inherently interrelated to other disciplines. Architecture's "relatedness" derives from its three geometries: compositional, projective and signified. Compositional geometry is haptic and stable, antique and earth-measured, frozen in form. Projective geometry is optic and destabilizing; the lines of sight embedded in Renaissance perspective undermine formal compositional geometry due to the moving body and eyes of the observer. Signified geometry is reflective and interpretive. For example, in the twentieth century architects attempted to metaphorically give form to new non-Euclidean geometries, higher mathematics and the uncertainty of Einsteinian relativity. Evans locates within these zones of instability - the interstices between building composition, an observing body, and self-conscious reflection - the projective cast of architecture. In *The Projective Cast*, Evans continually shows us "… the difference between forms of thought and forms of things." A centralized Renaissance church, contrary to common historical argument, does not appear unified, universal, or stable. Instead, its form reveals "embarrassing contradictions" between ideal compositional geometries and the optical perception of moving bodies in space. "Although unity was presupposed, and although all were convinced that perfect geometrical construction lay behind the diverse forms of the world, the excesses and defects, paradoxes and anomalies obtruded, so that if the principle held in one respect it failed in another."

In contrast Evans describes the fragmentary forms of the contemporary architectural avant-garde as merely an image of instability presented for a highly controlled and predictable western world.

For Guattari, repressive power is internalized by the oppressed, whose vision of the world is drained of the significance of human interventions. Troubled communities become apathetic and delegate the task of governing or managing society to others – such as architects and planners -allied with the productive-economic subjective assemblage of what he calls Integrated World Capitalism. A framework for urban patch dynamics would overlay Guattari's three ecologies and Evans' three geometries as a multi-scalar field of action within the economic and ecological phase space of the contemporary city. Ecological fluxes – mental, social, and environmental - are put in relation to the assumed stability of architecture until confronted by the mobile, self conscious observer. Urban designs as models of patch dynamics follow an "eco-logic of intensities" concerned only with evolutive processes, not system or structure, "...to capture existence in the very act of its constitution and definition." Paraphrasing Guattari, by means of transversal tools, subjectivity is able to install itself simultaneously in the realms of the environment, the major social and institutional assemblages, and in the landscapes and fantasies of the most intimate spheres of the individual psyche. The reconquest of a degree of creative autonomy in one particular domain encourages conquests in other domains – the catalyst for a gradual reforging and renewal of humanity's confidence in itself, starting at the most miniscule level. Urban design becomes an existential production engaged in processes of heterogenesis. Guattari's meta-modelization is distinctive in the way it develops possible openings into virtual and creative processes. Urban designs as models of patch dynamics would deploy the embodied and imaginative experience of Evan's three geometries of architecture within the circuits of Guattari's three ecologies, as a counter to the "fatalistic passivity" of mediated experience.

Conclusion

This book and the projects contained within imagine how architects might begin to incorporate patch dynamic theory in order to radically redirect architecture and urban design practice in a new field between ecology and design. The call to make urban designs models of patch dynamics resonates both institutionally and publicly. It demands innovative ways of teaching and thinking in the university, as well as challenges urban society to create new resilient city models as scientific and cultural eco-aesthetic experiments. While our sprawling fragmentary urban systems may reflect our democratic society, consumerist values, and desires for individuality, freedom and mobility, we need to search for tools to re-imagine cities as the symbolic order of human existence (Perez-Gomez 1986). Sustainable cities will not be achieved through greater technical or scientific knowledge alone; urban designs are needed to put the meaning of ecological theory into cultural practice. Contemporary architecture has successfully taken the human psyche as one of its primary sites of interest. Making urban design models of patch dynamics is part of a fuller urban eco-aesthetic approach. It fosters new forms of being in the world by extending ecology and architecture to embrace a renewal of social life and the environment in addition to the individual psyche. The projects presented here share an interest and optimism in the innate human ability to adjust to complex change, given the right access to education and information – and time.

References

Arrighi, Giobanni. 1994. The Long Twentieth Century. London: Verso.

Berrizbeitia, Anita. 2002. Scales of Undecidability. CASE: Downsview Park Toronto. Julia Czerniak, editor. Cambridge, MA: Harvard Graduate School of Design. 117-118.

Castells, Manuel. 1999. The Culture of Cites in the Information Age. Available from: http://www.arch. columbia.edu/Buell/mmarchive/s_2001/castells/castells_fs.html

Evans, Robin. 1995. The Projective Cast. Cambridge: MIT Press, Cambridge.

Genosko, Gary. 2002. Felix Guattari: Towards a Transdisciplinary Metamethodology. Angelaki 8: 1.

Guattari, Felix. 2000. The Three Ecologies. London: Athlone Press.

Johnson, Steven. 2001. Emergence. New York: Simon & Schuster.

Krugman, Paul. 1996. The Self Organizing Economy. Malden, MA: Blackwell Publishers.

Levin, Simon. 1999. Fragile Dominion. Cambridge, MA: Helix Books, Perseus Publishing.

Perez-Gomez, Alberto. 1986. The City as a Paradigm of Symbolic Order. Ottawa: Carleton University School of Architecture.